Coleção Eu gosto m@is

ENSINO FUNDAMENTAL

Edgar Laporta

INGLÊS

7º ano

1ª EDIÇÃO
SÃO PAULO
2012

IBEP

Coleção Eu Gosto Mais
Inglês 7º ano
© IBEP, 2012

Diretor superintendente	Jorge Yunes
Gerente editorial	Célia de Assis
Editor	Angelo Gabriel Rozner
Assistente editorial	Fernanda dos Santos Silva
Revisão técnica	Mariett Regina R. de Azevedo
Revisão	Rachel Prochoroff Castanheira
Coordenadora de arte	Karina Monteiro
Assistente de arte	Marilia Vilela
	Tomás Troppmair
Coordenadora de iconografia	Maria do Céu Pires Passuello
Assistente de iconografia	Adriana Neves
	Wilson de Castilho
Ilustrações	José Luis Juhas
Produção editorial	Paula Calviello
Produção gráfica	José Antônio Ferraz
Assistente de produção gráfica	Eliane M. M. Ferreira
Projeto gráfico e capa	Departamento de arte IBEP
Editoração eletrônica	Formato Comunicação

CIP-BRASIL. CATALOGAÇÃO-NA-FONTE
SINDICATO NACIONAL DOS EDITORES DE LIVROS, RJ

L32i

Laporta, Edgar
    Inglês : 7º ano / Edgar Laporta. - 1.ed. - São Paulo : IBEP, 2012.
    il. ; 28 cm.   (Eu gosto mais)

    ISBN 978-85-342-3445-0 (aluno) - 978-85-342-3449-8 (mestre)

    1. Língua inglesa - Estudo e ensino (Ensino fundamental). I. Título. II. Série.

12-6211   CDD: 372.6521
                                                      CDU: 373.3.016=111

28.08.12   05.09.12   038546

1ª edição - São Paulo - 2012
Todos os direitos reservados

IBEP

Av. Alexandre Mackenzie, 619 - Jaguaré
São Paulo - SP - 05322-000 - Brasil - Tel.: (11) 2799-7799
www.editoraibep.com.br   editoras@ibep-nacional.com.br

Impressão Serzegraf - Setembro 2016

Apresentação

O inglês é um idioma de grande importância no mundo globalizado de hoje. Está presente em nossa vida diária, na TV, no cinema, na Internet, nas músicas, nos livros, nas revistas etc.

Há muito tempo, tornou-se um dos principais meios de comunicação no turismo, no comércio mundial, nas competições esportivas, nos congressos sobre ciência e tecnologia, nos meios diplomáticos, nos encontros de líderes mundiais etc. Por isso, cada vez mais pessoas estudam e falam inglês.

Com o objetivo de despertar em você o gosto pelo idioma inglês, tivemos a preocupação de abordar textos variados e que se relacionam com sua vida.

As atividades de interpretação dos textos levam você a ler e reler o texto para encontrar as respostas adequadas às perguntas.

Sempre que você tiver alguma dificuldade em descobrir o sentido de palavras ou expressões do texto, lembre-se de que há no final do livro o vocabulário geral para ajudá-lo.

As noções de gramática são apresentadas na seção *Learn this* de forma simples e abreviada. Logo a seguir, você vai treiná-las com exercícios rápidos e simples.

Participe ativamente das aulas e aproveite esta oportunidade para aprender inglês.

O autor

Sumário

Lesson 1 – Affirmative form of imperative; possessive adjectives 7

Dialogue: *A new driver* 7
   Text comprehension 8
   Learn this 8
   Activities 9
   Learn this 10
Dialogue: *Asking directions* 10
   Role-play – oral drill 11
   Fun time 12

Lesson 2 – Negative form of imperative; why, because 13

Dialogue: *Some dangerous situations* 13
   Text comprehension 14
   Learn this 14
   Activities 15
   Fun time 17
   Listen and write – dictation 19
   Role-play – oral drill 19

Lesson 3 – Simple present tense of ordinary verbs 20

Texts: *Julia's daily actions* 20
   Text comprehension 22
   Learn this 23
   Activities 24
   Fun time 27

   Listen and write – dictation 30
   Review 30

Lesson 4 – Present tense; present continuous 32

Text: *What is Jack doing?* 32
   Text comprehension 34
   Learn this 35
   Activities 36
   Role-play – oral drill 39

Lesson 5 – Immediate future (near future) 40

Dialogue: *Teacher's day* 40
   Text comprehension 42
   Learn this 43
   Activities 43
   Fun time 45

Lesson 6 – Who are you? What do you do? 46

Text: *What is your job?* 46
Dialogue: *An interview* 48
   Text comprehension 49
   Learn this 49
   Activities 52
   Fun time 54
   Let's sing 55
   Review 55

Lesson 7 – Days of the week; prepositions in, on, at 57

Dialogue: *Lucy goes to a party* 57
- Text comprehension 58
- Learn this 58
- Activities 60

Dialogue: *An invitation* 62
- Text comprehension 62

Lesson 8 – Seasons and weather 64

Dialogue: *I prefer summer time* 65
- Text comprehension 65

Text: *The weather* 65
- Text comprehension 66
- Learn this 67
- Activities 68
- Role-play – oral drill 69
- Let's sing 69

Lesson 9 – Verb to have; let's, let us, too, no 70

Dialogue: *Let's enjoy life* 70
- Text comprehension 71
- Learn this 72
- Activities 73
- Fun time 74
- Let's sing 74

Dialogue: *Vacation in Rio* 75
- Text comprehension 75

Text: *After a week* 76
- Text comprehension 76

Lesson 10 – Past tense of verb to be and verb there to be 77

Text: *In those days* 77
- Text comprehension 78
- Learn this 79
- Activities 80

Lesson 11 – Interrogative words 82

Dialogue: *In a job agency* 82
- Text comprehension 83
- Learn this 84
- Activities 85

Lesson 12 – Plural of nouns 88

Dialogue: *Fair on Sampson Street* 88
- Text comprehension 90
- Learn this 90
- Activities 91
- Fun time 93

Lesson 13 – Plural os nouns 94

Text: *Charle's farm* 94
- Text comprehension 95
- Learn this 95
- Activities 96
- Fun time 97

Lesson 14 – Prepositions 99
Text: *The living room* 99
- Text comprehension 100
- Learn this 101
- Activities 102
- Review 102
- Fun time 104
- Let's sing 104

Lesson 15 – Genitive case 105
Dialogue: *Is it good to live in a apartment?* 105
- Text comprehension 106
- Learn this 107
- Activities 107

Lesson 16 – Possessive: his, her 108
Dialogue: *Diana's bedroom* 108
- Illustrated vocabulary 109
- Text comprehension 110
- Review 110

Dialogue: *Jim's bedroom* 112
- Illustrated vocabulary 113
- Text comprehension 113
- Learn this 114
- Activities 115
- Let's sing 115

Lesson 17 – Possessive adjectives ... 116
Dialogue: *In a tour agency* 116
- Text comprehension 119
- Learn this 119
- Activities 120
- Fun time 122
- Let's sing 123

General vocabulary 124

Lesson 1

AFFIRMATIVE FORM OF IMPERATIVE; POSSESSIVE ADJECTIVES

A new driver

Son: Father, let's fasten our seat belts, and let's go to visit my friend Joe.

Father: Son, be careful! One hundred and ten kilometers per hour! Drive slowly. Obey the traffic laws!

Son: You're right, dad. Excuse me...

Father: Pay attention, son! Stop the car! The traffic light is red.

TEXT COMPREHENSION

1 Is the son an attentive driver?

_____

2 The son and his father are going
   ( ) to a farm
   ( ) to a beach
   ( ) to visit a friend

3 What's the name of the friend they are going to visit?

_____

4 The father asks his son:
   ( ) to fasten the seat belt   ( ) to drive slowly
   ( ) to obey the traffic laws   ( ) to drive fast
   ( ) to pay attention   ( ) to stop the car
   ( ) to admire nature   ( ) to listen to the whistle of the train

6 At a certain moment, the young driver drives his car at a speed of
   ( ) sixty kilometers per hour
   ( ) one hundred kilometers per hour
   ( ) one hundred and ten kilometers per hour

LEARN THIS

IMPERATIVE (AFFIRMATIVE FORM)

1. O imperativo indica uma ordem, um pedido ou um conselho.

Stop the car! (Pare o carro!)

Drive slowly, please! (Dirija devagar, por favor!)

Em inglês, forma-se o imperativo retirando-se a partícula **to** do infinitivo:

Infinitivo: **To drive** (Dirigir)

Imperativo: **Drive.** (Dirija.)

Infinitivo: **To run** (Correr)

Imperativo: **Run!** (Corra!)

2. A palavra **please** significa por favor e é usada com o imperativo para transmitir uma ordem, pedido ou conselho de forma delicada e educada. Pode vir no começo ou no fim da frase. Quando vem no fim, é separada por vírgula.

Drive slowly, please. (Dirija devagar, por favor.)

Please shut the door. (Por favor, feche a porta.)

ACTIVITIES

1 Write in the imperative form:

a) to fasten your seat belt _____

b) to drive slowly _____

c) to obey the traffic laws _____

d) to go home _____

e) to pay attention _____

f) to stop the car _____

g) to show your documents _____

h) to take off your coat _____

2 Look at the example and use the word please in the imperative form:

a) **Obey the traffic laws.** **Please obey the traffic laws. Obey the traffic laws, please.**

b) Stand up. _____

c) Write your surname. _____

d) Read on page sixty. _____

3 Translate these imperative sentences:

a) Sit down, please. _____

b) Please close your book. _____

c) Come back to your place. _____

d) Put your schoolbag on that table. _____

e) Listen to the whistle of the train. _____

f) Go to the airport. _____

4 Write in English:

a) Escreva seu nome aqui, por favor. _____

b) Você está certo. _____

c) Por favor, preste atenção! _____

d) Dirija para o aeroporto, por favor. _____

LEARN THIS

Personal pronouns	Possessive adjectives	
I	my	(meu, minha, meus, minhas)
you	your	(seu, sua)
he	his	(dele)
she	her	(dela)
it	its	(dele/dela)
we	our	(nosso, nossa, nossos, nossas)
you	your	(seus, suas)
they	their	(deles, delas)

My house is small. (Minha casa é pequena.)
It is your radio. (É seu rádio.)
This is his ball. (Esta é sua bola. Esta é a bola dele.)
Her house is new. (Sua casa é nova. A casa dela é nova.)
This is a giraffe. Its neck is long. (Esta é uma girafa. Seu pescoço é longo.)
Our teacher is nice. (Nosso professor é ótimo/bacana/simpático.)
Your books are on the table. (Seus livros estão sobre a mesa.)
Their house is modern. (A casa deles/delas é moderna.)

Asking directions

Jessy: Excuse me, can you tell me where the Bank of America is?

Policeman: Sure. It's easy. Follow Florida Street. Go ahead for two blocks until Kennedy Street. On Kennedy Street turn right and then turn left.
The Bank of America is at 75 Nevada Street.

Jessy: Thank you.

Word bank

go ahead: vá em frente
turn right: vire à direita
turn left: vire à esquerda

ROLE-PLAY – ORAL DRILL

Um(a) aluno(a) ou o professor dita as ordens, enquanto os(as) alunos(as) escolhidos(as) as executam.

a) Please raise your hands.
   Put one hand down.
   Put the other hand down.
   Please open your book.
   Close your book.
   Close your hands.
   Open your hands.
   Raise your book.
   Put your book down.

b) Please touch your eyes.
   Touch your nose.
   Touch your foot.
   Touch your head.
   Touch your ear.
   Touch your right hand.
   Touch your left hand.
   Touch your left shoulder.
   Touch your right shoulder.

c) Go to the door, please.
   Walk slowly.
   Open the door.
   Close the door.
   Go to the blackboard.
   Write your name.
   Erase your name, please.
   Thank you. Sit down, please.

d) Please say good morning.
   Please say good night.
   Show your left arm.
   Show your right arm.
   Please say hello.
   Please say good bye.

eleven 11

FUN TIME

A driving school

Complete the story using the words or expressions in the box below:

the car – look at – my car! – belt – pay my fruit – drive

Fasten your seat _____, Mr Stone. _____ the car slowly.

Stop! Stop _____, Mr Stone!

Hey! Come back! _____, you awful driver!

_____ You awful driver!

Lesson 2
Negative form of imperative; why, because

Some dangerous situations

Friend: Don't smoke, my friend, because it's dangerous. Tobacco can cause cancer.

Mother: Don't throw garbage in the street! Throw the garbage in the wastebasket!

Coach: Don't be violent in the game! You can hurt someone. It's not fair to play this way.

Boy: Don't speak to the driver!
Girl: Why not?
Boy: Because you may distract his attention.

Word bank

garbage: lixo
wastebasket: cesta de lixo
fair: justa(o), honesta(o)
driver: motorista

TEXT COMPREHENSION

Answer according to the texts:

1 Is it dangerous to smoke?

( ) Yes, it is. ( ) No, it is not.

– Why?

_____

2 An educated person throws garbage:

( ) in the street. ( ) in the wastebasket.

3 Is it fair to play games with violence?

_____

– Why?

_____

4 – Why passengers must not speak to the driver?

_____

LEARN THIS

1. Imperative – negative form

Para formar o imperativo negativo, em Inglês, basta retirar a partícula **to** do infinitivo do verbo e colocar a expressão **don't** no seu lugar.

Observe:

To smoke: (Fumar) **Don't smoke!** (Não fume!)

To run: (Correr) **Don't run!** (Não corra!)

2. Please

A palavra **please** significa por favor. É usada com o imperativo para indicar delicadeza na maneira de dar ordens ou fazer pedidos. Pode vir no começo ou no fim da frase; se vier no final da frase é precedida de vírgula.

Don't smoke, please.

Please don't smoke.

3. Why...? / Because...

Why significa por que. É usado em perguntas. **Because** significa porque. É usado em respostas.

Observe:

Why is it dangerous to smoke? (Por que é perigoso fumar?)

Because tobacco can cause cancer. (Porque o tabaco pode provocar câncer.)

ACTIVITIES

1 Write sentences according to the example.

a) Sidney – shout – speak in a low voice.   Sidney, don't shout! Speak in a low voice.

b) Jane – run – walk normally   _____

c) Ronald – drive fast – drive slowly   _____

d) Marcel – smile – be serious   _____

e) Jessica – move – be quiet   _____

f) Flavia – watch TV – go to bed   _____

2 Look at the pictures and answer the question using the answers in the box:

> She's happy because the sandwich is big. She's hungry.
> He's sad because he has bad marks.
> She's angry because her son is dirty.
> He's is worried because he's late for school.

a) Why is Sandy angry?

b) Why is Sara happy?

c) Why is he sad?

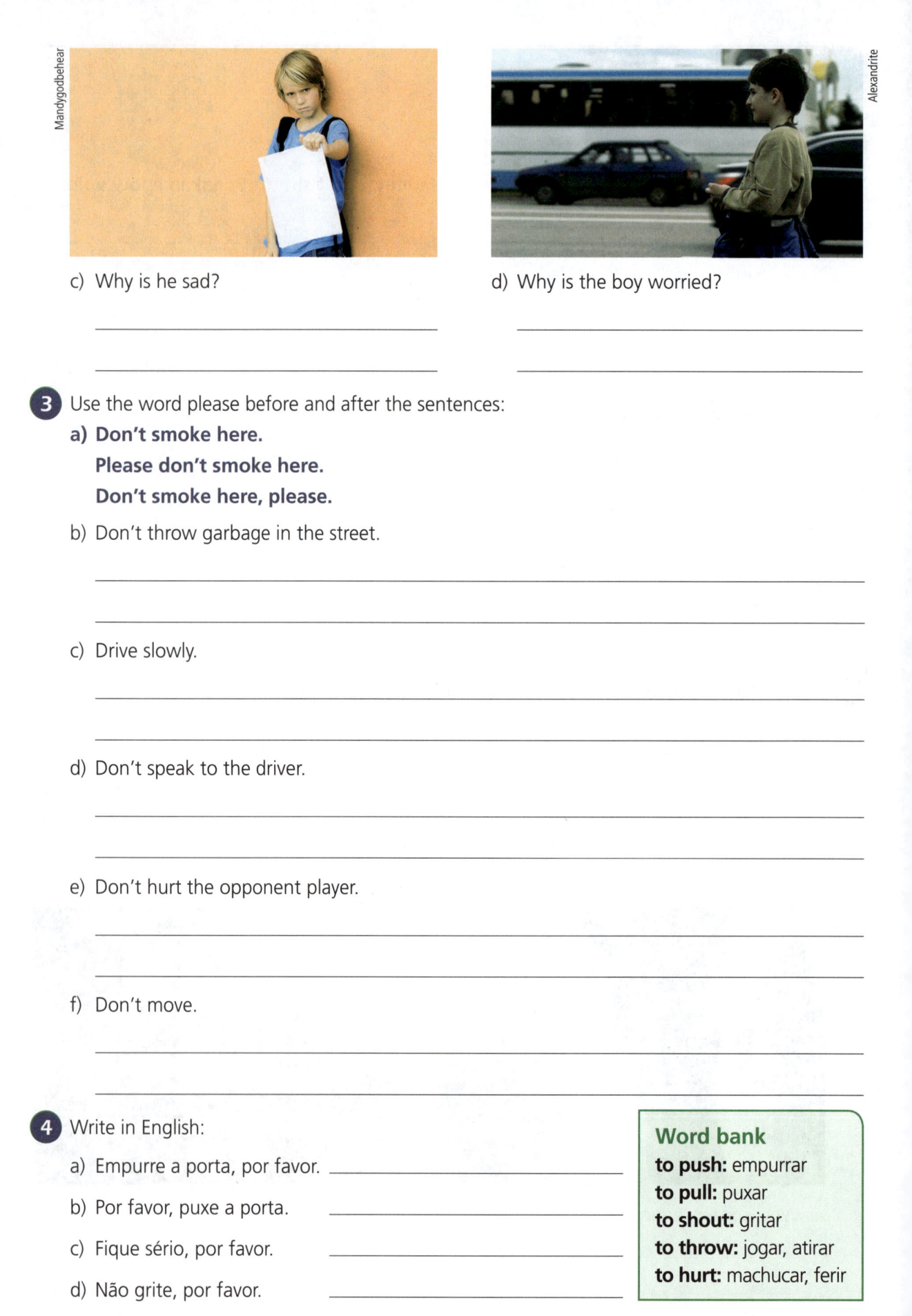

_____

_____

d) Why is the boy worried?

_____

_____

3 Use the word please before and after the sentences:

a) **Don't smoke here.**
   Please don't smoke here.
   Don't smoke here, please.

b) Don't throw garbage in the street.

_____

_____

c) Drive slowly.

_____

_____

d) Don't speak to the driver.

_____

_____

e) Don't hurt the opponent player.

_____

_____

f) Don't move.

_____

_____

4 Write in English:

a) Empurre a porta, por favor. _____

b) Por favor, puxe a porta. _____

c) Fique sério, por favor. _____

d) Não grite, por favor. _____

Word bank
to push: empurrar
to pull: puxar
to shout: gritar
to throw: jogar, atirar
to hurt: machucar, ferir

FUN TIME

1 Imperative crossword
1. Chame
2. Coma
3. Dirija
4. Venha
5. Responda
6. Leia
7. Brinque, jogue
8. Pegue
9. Espere

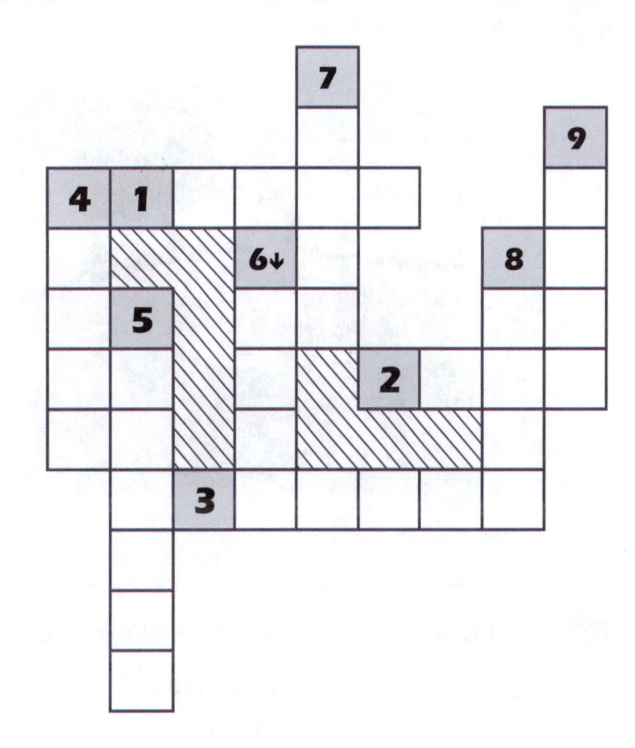

2 Write these orders in the respective balloons:

Don't smoke!
Don't smoke here!
Don't speak loud, please!
Don't write on the wall!

3 Translate the advice.

___

4 What can you see in the picture above? I can see:

( ) a tree ( ) a newspaper ( ) a lamp
( ) a cow ( ) a bench ( ) a boy
( ) a man ( ) a girl ( ) a little fence
( ) a house ( ) a warning ( ) a dog

___

5 Did the man in the picture above obey the advice?
( ) yes ( ) no

6 Rearrange the words and answer the question:
Why are the boys laughing at the man?
(Por que os meninos estão rindo do homem?)

is – getting – because wet – all – he

LISTEN AND WRITE – DICTATION

Throw _____ in the _____

_____ here, please.

_____ don't speak _____

_____ running?

I am worried _____

ROLE-PLAY – ORAL DRILL

You and a classmate.

Sob a orientação do professor, você e um(a) colega podem ir à frente da classe e encenar um diálogo. O(a) colega vai lhe perguntar se você lhe permite fazer algumas coisas, e você vai lhe dizer que não. Use o imperativo negativo.

Classmate: Can I sing here? (Começa a cantar).

You: No, don't sing here, please.

Classmate: Can I run here? (Ameaça correr).

You: No, don't run here, please.

Classmate: Can I open the door? (Ameaça abrir a porta).

You: No, don't open the door, please.

Classmate: Can I open the window? (Faz gesto de abrir a janela).

You: No, don't open the window, please.

Classmate: Can I write on the blackboard? (Vai escrever no quadro).

You: No, don't write on the blackboard, please.

Classmate: Can I sit on the table? (Vai sentar na mesa).

You: No, don't sit on the table, please.

Lesson 3
SIMPLE PRESENT TENSE OF ORDINARY VERBS

Julia's daily actions

Julia goes to bed early because she gets up early, too. She goes to bed at 9:30 p.m. She gets up at 7, makes her bed, washes her face, combs her hair and has her breakfast.

At breakfast she has coffee with milk and bread with butter.

At 7:30 Julia takes the bus to school. The school is near her house. She arrives at school at five to eight.

From 8 o' clock to 10 o' clock Julia has English and History lessons.

From 10 to 10:30 she has recess. During recess, Julia has her lunch and plays with her classmates. From 10:30 to 12 o'clock Julia has Science and Portuguese lessons.

At midday the lessons finish and Julia returns home.

At home, she takes her lunch, gets some rest and does her homework.

When Julia finishes her homework, she talk with her friends on the computer about many subjects. At 7:30, Julia takes a shower, has her dinner, watches some TV programs and goes to bed.

TEXT COMPREHENSION

Answer according to Julia's daily actions:

1 Julia goes to bed

( ) early.   ( ) late.

– Why?

_____

2 Write under the pictures what the persons are doing.

_____   _____

_____   _____

3 Julia goes to school

( ) by bus.   ( ) by car.   ( ) on foot.

4 Is Julia's house near or far from her school?

_____

5 Before the recess time, Julia has two lessons. What are they?

_____

6 And after the recess time, what are her lessons?

_____

LEARN THIS
SIMPLE PRESENT TENSE

1. O **simple present tense** (tempo presente simples) indica uma ação que se faz costumeiramente, ações habituais.
She makes her bed every day.
Ela arruma sua cama todos os dias.
Pode também descrever verdades universais e estado permanente das pessoas:
The wind blows. Man thinks. The Earth revolves around the Sun.
wash – washes: She washes her face
                 Ela lava seu rosto.
We need water to live.
Nós precisamos de água para viver.
We live in Brazil.
Nós moramos no Brasil.

2. Conjugação do verbo **to like** (gostar) no **simple present tense**:

Verb to like			
I like	(eu gosto)	It likes	(ele/ela gosta)
You like	(Você gosta)	We like	(nós gostamos)
He likes	(ele gosta)	You like	(vocês gostam)
She likes	(ela gosta)	They like	(eles/elas gostam)

A única modificação ocorre na 3ª pessoa do singular, em que o verbo geralmente recebe **s**.

3. Verb to have (ter, possuir)

O verbo **to have** (ter) apresenta a forma **has** nas 3ªs pessoas do singular (**he**, **she**, **it**).
He
She ——— has
It

4. Os verbos terminados por **s**, **sh**, **ch**, **o** e **x** recebem **es** nas terceiras pessoas do singular (he, she, it):
pass – passes: **He passes the ball.**   go – goes: **She goes to school in the morning.**
                 Ele passa a bola.   Ela vai para a escola de manhã.
wash – washes: **She washes her face.**   fix – fixes: **The mechanic fixes cars.**
                 Ela lava o rosto.   O mecânico conserta carros.
watch – watches: **He watches TV at night.**
                 Ele assiste à TV à noite.

5. Verbos terminados por **y**:
a) precedidos de vogal, acrescenta-se apenas **s**:
play – plays: **She plays basketball.**
                 Ela joga basquete.
b) precedidos de consoante perdem o **y** e recebem **ies**:
study – stydies: **He studies at night.**
                 Ele estuda à noite.

ACTIVITIES

1 Complete the sentences using the verbs in the present tense:

a) Julia _____ to school by bus. (go)

b) She _____ at seven o'clock. (get up)

c) The lesson _____ at 8 o'clock. (start)

d) The students _____ home at twelve o'clock. (come back)

e) She _____ her homework in the afternoon. (do)

f) My father _____ TV after dinner. (watch)

g) My sister _____ to bed at ten o'clock. (go)

h) Jenny _____ George. (love)

i) They _____ in a supermarket. (work)

j) He _____ English well. (speak)

2 Complete the text writing the verbs in the present tense, third person, singular:

to finish	to work
to get up	to have
to start	to protect
to take	to sleep

Edson Bliss _____ for a Protection Group. He _____ the members of the Kidman family and their employees. He _____ his work at four o'clock in the afternoon and _____ at midnight. He _____ from midnight to seven in the morning. He _____ at seven, _____ a shower and then _____ his breakfast.

24 twenty-four

3 Rewrite the sentences in the correct order under the appropriate pictures:

a) These – love – girls – to swim

b) This – an – woman – for – works – company – international

_____   _____

4 Write sentences in the third person, singular. Follow the pattern.

a) **Julia – to get up – early.** **Julia gets up early.**

b) The dog – to play – with a ball. _____

c) My mother – to start – her work at 9. _____

d) My father – to watch – TV after dinner. _____

e) Rosie – to take – a shower in the morning. _____

5 Write the sentences in the plural. Follow the pattern.

a) **I work in an office.** **We work in an office (in offices).**

b) She dances very well. _____

c) He is a good soccer player. _____

d) She speaks English. _____

e) He drinks a lot of water. _____

f) She has breakfast at 7. _____

g) The cat plays with a ball. _____

6 Write in English:

a) Ela se levanta às sete horas. _____

b) Ele trabalha para uma companhia inglesa. _____

7 Write about your routine from Monday to Saturday.

Use the expressions in the box and write in each clock the time you are doing the actions:

> I get up at
> I have dinner at
> I begin school at
> I go to school at
> I finish school at
> I do my homework at
> I go to bed at
> I play with my computer at
> I have breakfast at

FUN TIME

Imperative crossword

1 Complete the sentences and the crosswords translating the verbs in parenthesis:

1. _____ aloud! (Fale)
2. _____ the thief! (Pegue)
3. _____ the door! (Feche)
4. _____ a moment! (Espere)
5. _____ the window! (Abra)
6. _____ your teeth! (Escove)
7. _____ hard! (Trabalhe)
8. _____ your hands! (Lave)
9. _____ the car! (Pare)
10. _____ the work! (Comece)

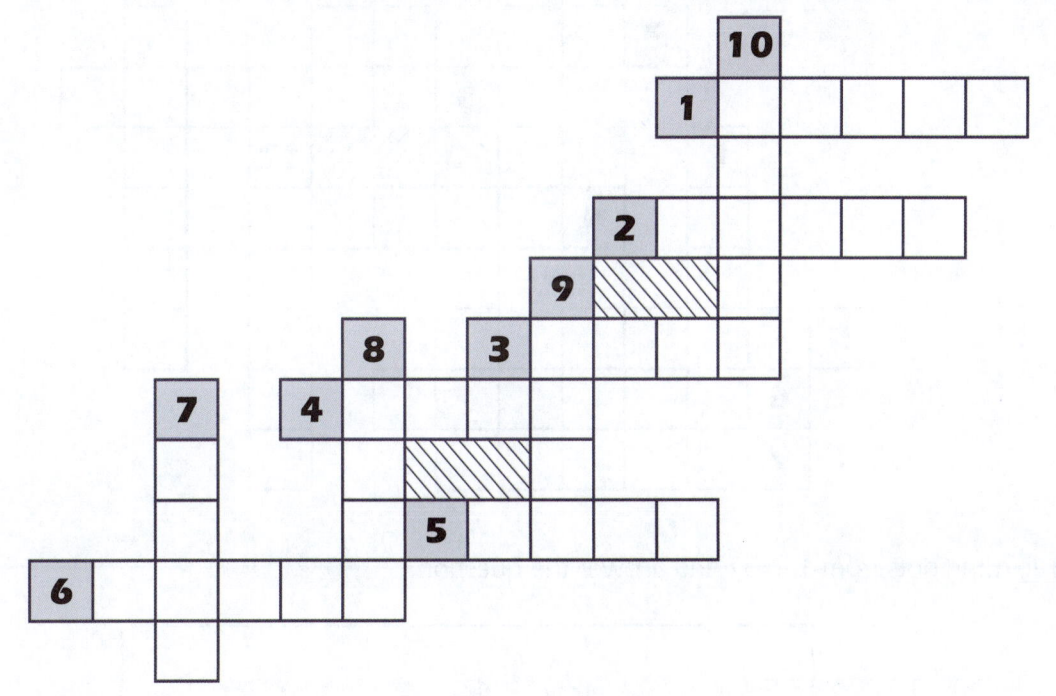

2 Complete the sentences and the crossword using the verbs in the third person, singular:

1. (to like) – John _____ tennis.
2. (to love) – Mary _____ me.
3. (to sleep) – Ted _____ late every night.
4. (to stop) – He _____ the car.
5. (to eat) – Lee _____ rice every day.
6. (to dance) – Rose _____ every weekend.
7. (to sing) – The bird _____ well.
8. (to read) – Jim _____ magazines every week.
9. (to come) – David _____ late every day.

twenty-seven **27**

10. (to take) – She _____ the bus every morning.
11. (to live) – He _____ in Washington.
12. (to show) – He _____ me some pictures.
13. (to speak) – She _____ Japanese.

3 Join the dots from 1 to 37 and answer the question.

Is the man pushing or pulling the cart? _____

4 Find these words in the diagram:

take	fasten	girl	father
start	swim	window	drives

R	S	R	T	C	X	Z	A	T	U	O	D	R	I	V	E	S	U
A	F	T	C	X	O	B	E	O	V	X	A	R	E	C	F	L	K
V	A	C	Z	S	T	A	R	T	D	U	T	R	S	W	I	M	I
A	T	C	G	D	W	Y	U	O	P	E	A	D	C	R	B	N	S
D	H	G	H	K	I	U	T	R	E	Q	Z	X	C	B	N	H	O
X	E	B	H	U	N	B	V	C	T	A	K	E	R	T	E	Q	A
V	R	X	Z	D	D	G	R	E	A	E	U	P	O	U	R	B	N
G	I	R	L	Z	O	O	X	X	C	V	B	X	Z	W	I	N	D
V	X	C	B	N	W	X	D	F	A	S	T	E	N	V	V	C	X

5 What's the odd word?

odd: estranho, avulso, que não pertence ao grupo.

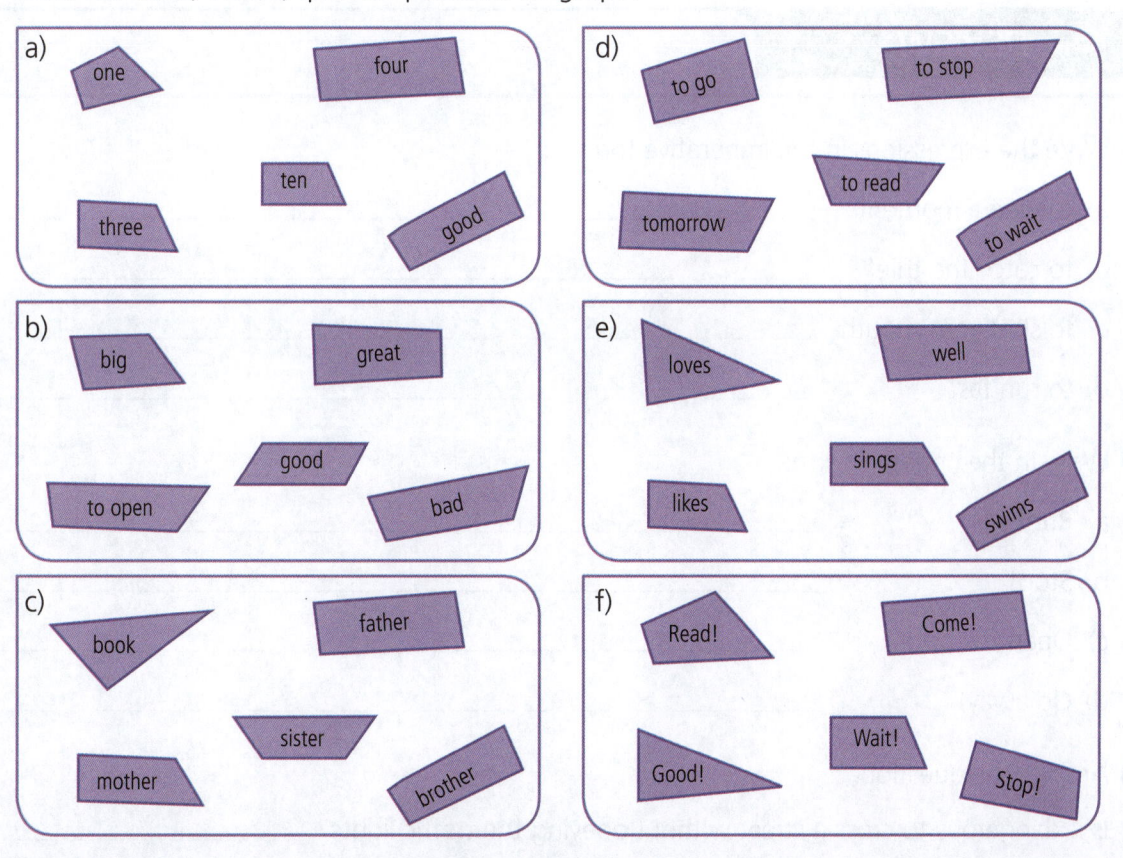

a) one, four, ten, three, good

b) big, great, good, to open, bad

c) book, father, sister, mother, brother

d) to go, to stop, to read, tomorrow, to wait

e) loves, well, sings, likes, swims

f) Read!, Come!, Wait!, Good!, Stop!

6 Challenge:

The missing words

Use your intelligence and fill in the blanks with the missing words:

a) One, three, five, _____

b) It isn't old; it's _____

c) Big – small; fast – slow; good – _____

d) To stand up – to sit down; to start – to finish; to go – to come; to close – to _____

e) To drive a car; to open a door; to write a letter; to _____ a book.

LISTEN AND WRITE – DICTATION

Julia _____ in the morning.

She _____, washes her face and _____ hair.

She _____ and goes to school, _____ house.

During the recess time, Julia _____ in the yard.

After midday, _____, has lunch and _____

REVIEW

1 Write the expressions in the imperative form:

a) to wait a moment   _____

b) to catch the thief   _____

c) to shut your mouth _____

d) to run fast   _____

2 Write in the negative form:

a) Run!   _____

b) Stop!   _____

c) Open the door! _____

d) Go away!   _____

3 Answer the question.

Is it dangerous to cross a street without obeying the traffic lights? _____

30 thirty

4 Turn to English:

a) Não fume aqui, por favor. _____

b) Espere um momento, por favor. _____

5 Translate:

a) Can you tell me where Palm Street is? _____

b) Go ahead for two blocks. _____

c) Sit down, please. _____

6 Write the sentences in the third person, singular:

a) I am very happy. _____

b) There are sharks near the beach.
_____
_____

c) We have lunch at midday. _____
_____

d) They start school at eight o'clock. _____
_____

7 Read about Jane and answer the questions:

Jane is ten years old. She lives in Miami but she is from Brazil. She goes to school near her house. The name of her school is Saint George. Her two brothers study at the same school. Her father works in a restaurant and her mother is a teacher of Portuguese for Americans. Jane is a very happy girl.

a) How old is Jane?
_____

b) Where is she from? _____

c) What's the name of her school? _____
_____

d) How many brothers does she have? _____

e) What's her father's occupation? _____
_____

thirty-one **31**

Lesson 4

PRESENT TENSE: PRESENT CONTINUOUS

What is Jack doing?

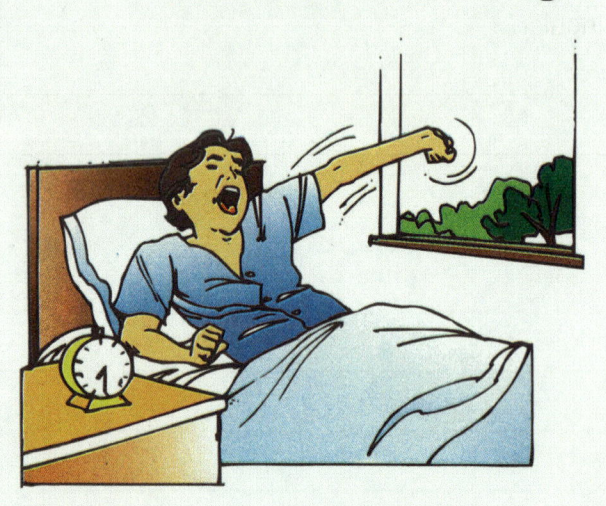

Jack is a lazy boy.
He is getting up now.
He gets up late every day.

Now he is having his breakfast. Every day, in the morning, he drinks coffee and milk and eats bread with butter.

Jack likes to play soccer.
He is playing soccer with Bob and Jim.

Look! Jack is going to school.
He goes to school in the afternoon.

Now Jack is coming back from school.
He comes back with Bob every day.

Jack is hungry.
He eats a lot.
Now he is eating a banana.

Jack is studying now.
He's studying English.
He studies in the evening.

Jack is tired.
He goes to bed late.
And now... he is sleeping.

TEXT COMPREHENSION

Look at the picture and answer according to the text.

a) What is Jack doing?

_____

b) Jack generally gets up:

   ( ) early   ( ) late

c) And now, what's he doing?

_____

d) What's Jack eating now?

_____

Jack eats:

   ( ) little   ( ) a lot

e) What's Jack doing?

_____

f) Where is Jack going to?

_____

g) He goes to school:

   ( ) in the morning.
   ( ) in the afternoon.

h) Where is Jack coming from?

_____

i) Who is coming back from school with Jack?

_____

j) What's Jack doing?

_____

k) What is Jack doing now?

_____

LEARN THIS

SIMPLE PRESENT TENSE

Jack **goes** to bed late every day.
(Jack dorme tarde todos os dias.)

Jack **plays** soccer every day.
(Jack joga futebol todos os dias.)

O **simple present** (presente simples) indica uma ação que se faz costumeiramente, que se repete normalmente.

Observe a conjugação do verbo **to sleep** (dormir) no presente simples.

PRESENT CONTINUOUS TENSE

Jack **is sleeping** now.
(Jack está dormindo agora.)

Jack **is playing** soccer now.
(Jack está jogando futebol agora.)

O **present continuous** (presente contínuo) indica uma ação que se está fazendo agora, que começou e continua ainda neste momento.

Observe a conjugação do mesmo verbo no presente contínuo.

SIMPLE PRESENT	PRESENT CONTINUOUS
I sleep (Eu durmo.)	**I am sleeping** (Eu estou dormindo.)
You sleep (Você dorme.)	**You are** sleeping
He sleeps (Ele dorme.)	**He is sleeping**
She sleeps (Ela dorme.)	**She is sleeping**
It sleeps	**It is sleeping**
We sleep (Nós dormimos.)	**We are sleeping**
You sleep (Vocês dormem.)	**You are sleeping**
They sleep (Eles(as) dormem.)	**They are sleeping**

Observações

O presente contínuo é formado pelo verbo **to be** (verbo estar) no presente + o gerúndio do verbo principal. Para formar o gerúndio, acrescentamos **ing** ao verbo; exemplo:

sleep – sleeping
play – playing
drink – drinking

ACTIVITIES

1 Change into gerund. Follow the model:

to read – reading   **to go – going**

to cook _____   to look _____

to teach _____   to study _____

2 Conjugate the verb to read in the present continuous tense:

I am reading (eu estou lendo)

You _____   We _____

He _____   You _____

She _____   They _____

3 Look at the pictures and complete the sentences with the verbs in the box. Use the present continuous tense:

> to plant   to eat   to read
> to sleep   to drink to study

a) The boys _____ the lesson.

b) The girl _____ milk.

c) The man _____ a newspaper.

d) Mary _____ an apple.

e) The baby _____

f) The girls _____ trees.

4 Answer the questions according to the example:

a) Are you reading a book? (magazine) **No, I'm not. I'm reading a magazine.**

b) Are you writing a letter? (story) _____

c) Are you working? (watching TV) _____

d) Is she studying Portuguese? (English) _____

5 Make questions using the interrogative words who and what.
Look at the example and do the same:

a) **Jessica is driving a car.**

Who is driving a car? Jessica is.

What is Jessica driving? She is driving a car.

b) Emilie is eating an apple.

_____
_____
_____
_____

6 Make questions for the answers in the balloons.
The questions are in the box:

Why are you working?   Why are you escaping?
Why is the dog running?   Why are you afraid?

I am afraid **because** there is a snake behind you!

Because it wants to catch the cat!

What are they doing?

7 Answer according to the pictures. Make the question and then answer it. Look at the example.

1. What's Mark doing?

He's running.

2. What's Jeff doing

He _____

3. What's Paul doing?

He _____

4. What's Diana doing?

She _____

ROLE-PLAY – ORAL DRILL

You and two classmates.

Você e mais dois colegas vão à frente da classe encenar as ações sugeridas, fazendo as perguntas e dando as respostas em inglês.

a) Você dará as ordens.
b) Um(a) colega vai executar as ordens.
c) Você dirige perguntas para outro(a) colega sobre o que está sendo executado.
d) Este(a) responde em inglês.

Veja alguns exemplos:

A

1. **You command**: **Please sing a song**.
2. Seu(sua) colega executa a ordem e canta.
3. **You ask to another classmate**: **What's he(she) doing**?
4. **The other classmate answer**: **He(she) is singing**.

B

1. **You command**: **Please open your book and read**.
2. Seu(sua) colega executa a ordem, abre um livro e finge que está lendo.
3. **You ask to another classmate**: **What's he(she) doing**?
4. **The other classmate answer**: **He(she) is reading a book**.

C

1. **You command**: **Please, write your name on the blackboard**.
2. Seu(sua) colega executa a ordem escrevendo o nome dele(a) na lousa.
3. **You ask to another classmate**: **What's he(she) doing**?
4. **The other classmate answer**: **He(she) is writing on the board**.

D

1. **You command**: **Please, go to the door**.
2. Seu(sua) colega executa a ordem e vai em direção à porta.
3. **You ask to another classmate**: **What's he(she) doing**?
4. **The other classmate answer**: **He(she) is going to the door.**

Lesson 5
IMMEDIATE FUTURE (NEAR FUTURE)

Teacher's Day

Natalie: Class, attention, please! Next Friday is Teacher's Day. What about a party to celebrate the date? The teachers deserve our recognition. Who agrees?

Class: I... I... I...

Natalie: OK! Everybody agrees with the party. We need some money to buy gifts for the teachers.
Who is going to contribute with some amount?

Class: I... I... I...

Natalie: OK! Everybody is going to contribute. Who is going to decorate the classroom with flowers and banners?

Jane and Carol: We are going to decorate the classroom.

Natalie: That's fine, girls! Who is going to bring some snacks, pies, popcorn?

Bill and Jim: We are going to bring snacks.

Natalie: OK, boys! Who is going to bring the cake?

Rose and Nicole: We are going to bring the cake.

Natalie: Thank you, girls! And who is going to bring the sodas?

Colin and Frank: We are going to bring the sodas.

Natalie: OK, boys! And finally who is going to bring glasses, napkins, spoons, towel and knives?

Josie and Diana: We are going to bring all these things.

Natalie: Thank you everybody. I think we are going to have a wonderful party!

TEXT COMPREHENSION

1 Answer the questions according to the text:

a) What's the name of the girl who is organizing a party for the teachers?
_____

b) What is the reason for the party?
_____

c) Does the class agree with the party?
_____

2 Write T for true and F for false:

a) Who is going to contribute with some amount of money?
Natalie is ( )
Jack and Carol ( )
Everybody ( )

b) Who is going to decorate the classroom?
Everybody ( )
Rose and Nicole ( )
Jane and Carol ( )

c) Who is going to bring snacks?
Bill and Jim ( )
Josie and Diana ( )
Natalie ( )

3 Write the names of some materials we need in a party:
_____

4 In the space below draw or glue some materials we need in a party:

LEARN THIS

IMMEDIATE FUTURE or NEAR FUTURE

O futuro imediato indica uma ação já determinada, que vai ser realizada imediatamente ou dentro de pouco tempo.

Observe:

I am going to decorate the room. (Eu vou enfeitar a sala.)

She is going to bring the cake. (Ela vai trazer o bolo.)

They are going to drink water. (Eles vão beber água.)

O futuro imediato é formado por:

am
is — **going** + infinitivo do verbo principal
are

I am going to drink water.   (Eu vou beber água.)
You are going to drink water. (Você vai beber água.)
He is going to drink water.   (Ele vai beber água.)
She is going to drink water. (Ela vai beber água.)
It is going to drink water.   (Ele/ela vai beber água.)
We are going to drink water. (Nós vamos beber água.)
You are going to drink water. (Vocês vão beber água.)
They are going to drink water.(Eles/elas vão beber água.)

ACTIVITIES

1 Observe the model and write the verbs in the immediate future and in the present continuous tense:

Immediate future

Present continuous tense

a) (Jane – going to watch TV)   (Now she – watching TV)
   Jane is going to watch TV.   Now she is watching TV.

forty-three 43

b) (Mary – going to swim)

_____

(Now she – swimming)

_____

c) (Paul – going to play soccer)

_____

(Now he – playing soccer)

_____

d) (Meg – going to read a letter)

_____

(Now she – reading the letter)

_____

e) (The boys – going to eat the cake)

_____

(Now they – eating the cake)

_____

2 Write the words in the correct order and form sentences:

a) to give – present – are going – a – we – teacher – to – the

_____

b) eating – cake – the – are – now – they

_____

c) snacks – to bring – going – are – we

_____

d) going – bring – who – is – glasses – the – to – ?

_____

44 forty-four

3 Make sentences using the immediate future:
   a) **Mary – to read a magazine.**
      Mary is going to read a magazine.

   b) They – to drink an orange juice.
   _____

   c) We – to cross the street.
   _____

   d) Chris – to visit a friend.
   _____

4 Make questions and then answer them:
   a) **(going to give a watch to the teacher – a book)**
      Are you going to give a watch to the teacher?
      No, I'm going to give a book.

   b) (going to celebrate the Independence Day – Teacher's Day)
   _____
   _____

   c) (going to decorate the bedroom – the living room)
   _____
   _____

   d) (going to bring some snacks – a cake)
   _____
   _____

FUN TIME

1 Find out five differences in the second picture.

I'm going to eat an ice-cream!

FROZEN YOGURT

I'm going to eat a yogurt!

2 What are the animals going to eat?
Connect the animal with its favorite food.

bone

grass

banana

fish

a) The monkey is going to eat a _____
b) The dog is going to eat a _____
c) The cat is going to eat a _____
d) The cow is going to eat _____

3 Who is going to read what?

a) Who is going to read the book?
( ) The boy ( ) The girl ( ) The man
b) Who is going to read the magazine?
( ) The boy ( ) The girl ( ) The man
c) Who is going to read the newspaper?
( ) The man ( ) The boy ( ) The girl

Is Jim going to catch a fish with a hammer?

46 forty-six

Lesson 6

Who are you?
What do you do?
What is your occupation?

What is your job?
What is she doing?
She is searching some data in the Internet about her job.
She's a shop manager.
She works for a famous shop in São Paulo. She's very efficient!

An interview

Reporter: Excuse me. May I ask you some questions?
Charles: Sure... what are they about?
Reporter: About your job.
Charles: Ok. I'm Charles. I'm an engineer. And you? What's your name? What's your occupation?
Reporter: My name's George. I'm a reporter. I interview people for the famous *News Week Magazine*. What are you building here, Charles?
Charles: Our company is building a stadium.
Reporter: Is it a private or a public stadium?
Charles: It's a public stadium.
Reporter: Is it a big or a small stadium?
Charles: Oh, it's a very big stadium!
Reporter: Is it expensive?
Charles: Oh, it is expensive, of course!
Reporter: When are you going to finish it?
Charles: We are going to finish this stadium next year.
Reporter: Congratulations! Thank you for this interview!
Charles: You're welcome!

TEXT COMPREHENSION

Answer the questions according to the text.

1 Who's the reporter?
_____

2 George works for
( ) a newspaper.
( ) a famous magazine.

3 Who's the engineer?
_____

4 What's Charles' company building?
_____

5 What kind of stadium is it?
_____

6 Is it a big stadium?
_____

7 Is the stadium cheap?
_____

8 When is Charles going to finish the stadium?
_____

LEARN THIS

Observe as expressões:

1. **Who are you?/What is your name?**
Usam-se essas expressões para se perguntar o nome de uma pessoa:
– **Who are you?/What is your name?**
– **I am Fred./My name is Fred.**

2. **What do you do?** (O que você faz)
Usa-se essa expressão para se perguntar qual a profissão, a ocupação, o emprego ou a atividade que uma pessoa exerce:
– **What do you do?**
– **I am a teacher**.

3. **What is your occupation?** (Qual é sua ocupação, profissão?)
– **I'm a driver.**

4. – What are you doing? (O que você está fazendo?)
   – I'm driving a car.
5. What are you going to do? (O que você vai fazer?)
6. Observação
   Alguns substantivos que indicam profissões originam-se de verbos e recebem o sufixo **er**:

Verb	Ocupations
to teach (ensinar)	**teacher** (professor)
to sing (cantar)	**singer** (cantor)
to drive (dirigir)	**driver** (motorista)
to paint (pintar)	**painter** (pintor)
to dance (dançar)	**dancer** (dançarino)
to work (trabalhar)	**worker** (operário)
to play (jogar)	**player** (jogador)
to write (escrever)	**writer** (escritor)
to run (correr)	**runner** (corredor)

Occupations (jobs)

I am Bill. I am a **gardener**.
I plant flowers.

John is a reporter. He writes texts for a newspaper.

Anne is a **cook**. She cooks very well.
She is in the kitchen.

Meg is an **artist**.
She likes to paint.

Betty is a **teacher**.
She likes to teach English.
She is an English teacher.

Julie is a good **doctor**.
She works in a big hospital.

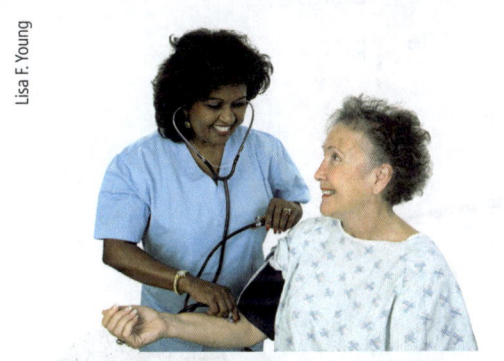

Nuria is a **nurse**.
She helps doctor Bob in the hospital.

Donald is a **farmer**.
He likes to live on the farm.

Jim is a **soccer player**.
He plays soccer.

Mr Benson is an **engineer**.
He builds houses.

Some other occupations:

tour guide	writer	dancer	policeman	manager
actor	mechanic	model	lawyer	housewife
actress	driver	firefighter	salesman	baker
maid	electrician	plumber	nurse	clerk

ACTIVITIES

1 Connect the verb to the occupation:

the cook • • teaches
the teacher • • plays
the painter • • cooks
the player • • sings
the singer • • paints
the farmer • • works
the worker • • builds
the engineer • • plants

2 Answer the questions:

a) Who **builds** houses?
( ) the doctor
( ) the engineer
( ) the player

b) Who **paints** houses?
( ) the cook
( ) the nurse
( ) the painter

c) Who **lives** on a farm?
( ) the singer
( ) the farmer
( ) the doctor

d) Who **works** in a factory?
( ) the worker
( ) the sailor
( ) the reporter

e) Who **plays** soccer?
( ) the nurse
( ) the secretary
( ) the soccer player

f) Who **works** in a hospital?
( ) the farmer
( ) the singer
( ) the doctor

3 Answer.

a) **Nancy / secretary**
Who are you?   I am Nancy.
What do you do?   I am a secretary.

b) **Katy / worker**
Who are you? _____
What do you do? _____

c) **Donald / farmer**
Who are you? _____
What do you do? _____

52 fifty-two

4 Follow the pattern:

a) **Bill – player – to play very well**   **Bill is a player. He plays very well.**

b) Fred – worker – to work every day _____

c) Charles – clerk – to sell books and magazines in a bookshop _____

d) Juliana – reporter – to write articles for a newspaper _____

5 Observe the model and make dialogues in your copybook:

a) **Mary – student – to study – in a – big school.**
   - **Who are you?**
   - **I am Mary.**
   - **What do you do?**
   - **I am a student.**
   - **I study in a big school.**

b) Paul – doctor – to work in a hospital

c) Betty – cashier – to work in a supermarket

d) Mark – inspector – to work in a big factory

e) Barbara – secretary – to work in a school

f) Frank – carpenter – to make chairs and tables

FUN TIME

Crosswords

1 Translate the occupations or professions

1. Secretária
2. Pintor
3. Médico
4. Repórter
5. Marinheiro
6. Enfermeira
7. Jardineiro

2 Translate the verbs and occupations

1. Pegando, tomando
2. Ajudar
3. Cozinheiro
4. Escrever
5. Bebendo
6. Jardineiro
7. Trabalhar
8. Professor
9. Garçom
10. Enfermeira
11. Marinheiro
12. Mostrando

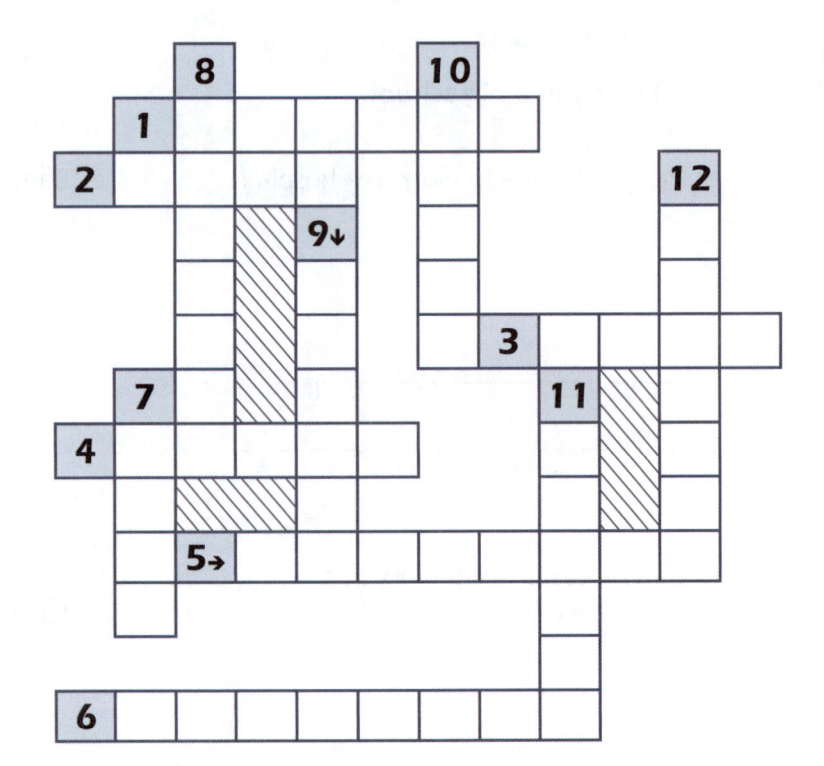

54 fifty-four

LET'S SING!

My father is a goog butcher.
My mother is a good teacher.
My sister is a film star!
My brother is a crazy boy:

he plays his guitar,
he thinks he is Jimmi Hendrix!
Oh! He thinks he is Jimmi Hendrix!
Ah, ah!

Antes de cantar a música, ouça o professor ou o CD, prestando atenção na pronúncia das palavras e procurando saber o significado delas. Jimmi Hendrix foi um famoso roqueiro e guitarrista americano dos anos 1960.

REVIEW

1 Write the gerund of these verbs:

a) **to drink – drinking**

b) to study – _____

c) to play – _____

d) to read – _____

e) to take – _____

f) to wait – _____

g) to wear – _____

2 Answer:

a) What are you eating? (an apple) _____
b) What are they drinking? (some milk) _____
c) What is he writing? (a story) _____
d) What is she reading? (a letter) _____

3 Follow the pattern:

a) **Where are you going now? (to school)**
   I am going to school. And you? Where are you going?
   I am going to school, too.

b) Where are you going now? (to church)
   _____
   _____

c) Where are you going now? (to the park)
   _____
   _____

fifty-five **55**

4 Follow the pattern:

a) (I – to the bookshop)   I am going to the bookshop.

b) (He – to the club)   _____

c) (She – to the library)   _____

d) (They – to the gas station)   _____

5 Follow the pattern:

a) (You – to see a film this evening)   You are going to see a film this evening.

b) (She – to buy a magazine)   _____

c) (They – to take a bus)   _____

d) (I – to write a letter)   _____

6 Follow the pattern:

a) John – painting a house? (a car)
Is John painting a house? No, he is not.
What is he doing? He is painting a car.

b) Mary – eating a banana? (an apple)

_____

_____

c) Peter – driving a car? (a bus)

_____

_____

d) They – drinking coffee? (water)

_____

_____

7 Complete the sentences with these words:

> soccer – player – singer – driver – teacher – English

a) Bill sings very well. He is a _____.

b) Bob drives fast. He is a _____.

c) Alan plays soccer every day. He is a _____.

d) Alice is teaching English. She is a _____.

Lesson 7

DAYS OF THE WEEK: PREPOSITIONS IN, ON, AT

Lucy goes to a party

Lucy receives a phone call inviting her to Grace's birthday tonight at seven o'clock.

Lucy: Dad, can I go to Grace's party today?

Dad: Of course, she's your best friend! Is it her birthday?

Lucy: Yeah!

Dad: Is Grace fifteen?

Lucy: No, she is fourteen.

Dad: What's she like?

Lucy: Grace's tall, beautiful and a very good student, too. Can you drive me there, dad? She lives near the school.

Dad: Sure. But be ready to come back at nine o'clock.

Lucy: At nine? Oh, no! It's too early. The party begins at seven!

Lucy: Can I come back at eleven?

Dad: Well, I think it's late. What about ten thirty?

Lucy: Big deal!

TEXT COMPREHENSION

1 What's Grace like?
_____

2 Where's Grace's house?
_____

3 Is Grace's party really today or tonight?
_____

4 For Lucy's father to be back from the party at 11 o'clock
( ) is too late.
( ) is too early.

5 And for Lucy to be back from the party at 9 o'clock
( ) is too late.
( ) is too early.

6 Lucy goes to Grace's party
( ) by car.
( ) by moto.
( ) by bus.

7 Who takes Lucy to Grace's party?
( ) her father.
( ) a boy.
( ) her mother.

8 How old is Grace? _____

LEARN THIS

1. Days of the week (Dias da semana)

Português	English
Domingo	**Sunday**
Segunda-feira	**Monday**
Terça-feira	**Tuesday**
Quarta-feira	**Wednesday**
Quinta-feira	**Thursday**
Sexta-feira	**Friday**
Sábado	**Saturday**

There are seven days in a week.

There are twenty-four hours in a day.

There are sixty minutes in an hour.

There are sixty seconds in a minute.

2. Prepositions of time

a)
Before (antes)	Saturday comes before Sunday. (Sábado vem antes de domingo.)
After (depois)	Monday comes after Sunday. (Segunda-feira vem depois de domingo.)

I have a shower before going to bed.
After dinner I usually watch TV.

b) **On – at**

Observe o emprego dessas preposições com os dias da semana (**on**) e com as horas (**at**):

On Saturday at six o'clock (Sábado às seis horas.)
On Friday evening (Sexta-feira à noite.)
On Sunday morning (Domingo de manhã.)
On Monday afternoon (Segunda-feira à tarde.)

Obs: Em inglês, os dias da semana são escritos com letra inicial maiúscula.

3. Veja o emprego das preposições **in** e **at** com relação aos períodos do dia:

In the morning: pela manhã   **At night**: à noite
In the afternoon: à tarde   **At midday**: ao meio-dia
In the evening: ao anoitecer   **At midnight**: à meia-noite

4. Quando se faz referencia a lugares subentendidos não é preciso mencioná-los.

Office: escritório ou consultório

I go to the dentist's. Eu vou ao consultório do dentista (está subentendido o termo office após o apóstrofo + **s**)

I am coming from the lawyer's. Estou voltando do escritório do advogado (está subentendido o termo **office** após o **'s**).

5. Observe o emprego a palavra **next**: próximo(a)

Next Sunday. (No próximo domingo.)
Next week. (Na próxima semana.)

6 **Verb there to be** (verbo haver, existir)

Verb there to be (affirmative form – Simple present)		
Simple present	There is (singular)	There is a party on Friday. (Há uma festa na sexta.)
Simple present	There are (plural)	There are flowers in the vase. (Há flores no vaso.)

Verb there to be (negative form – Simple present)		
Simple present	There isn't (singular)	There isn't a party on Friday. (Não há uma festa na sexta.)
Simple present	There aren't (plural)	There aren't flowers in the vase. (Não há flores no vaso.)

Verb there to be (interrogative form – Simple present)		
Simple present	Is there…? (singular)	Is there a party on Friday? (Há uma festa na sexta?)
Simple present	Are there…? (plural)	Are there flowers in the vase? (Há flores no vaso?)

ACTIVITIES

1 Answer:

a) How many days are there in a week?
_____

b) How many hours are there in a day?
_____

c) How many minutes are there in an hour?
_____

d) How many seconds are there in a minute?
_____

> **Let's learn:**
> **ORDINAL NUMBERS:**
>
> | | | | |
> |---|---|---|---|
> | 1st | first | 11th | eleventh |
> | 2nd | second | 12th | twelfth |
> | 3rd | third | 13th | thirteenth |
> | 4th | fourth | 14th | fourteenth |
> | 5th | fifth | 15th | fifteenth |
> | 6th | sixth | 16th | sixteenth |
> | 7th | seventh | 17th | seventeenth |
> | 8th | eighth | 18th | eighteenth |
> | 9th | ninth | 19th | nineteenth |
> | 10th | tenth | 20th | twentieth |

2 Follow the pattern:

a) (first – Monday)
What is the first day of the week?
The first day of the week is Sunday.

b) (second – Monday)
_____
_____

c) (fourth – Wednesday)
_____
_____

d) (sixth – Friday)
_____
_____

e) (today – Friday)
What day is today?
Today is Friday.

f) (today – Saturday)
_____
_____

g) (today – Sunday)
_____
_____

3 Write the days of the week in order beginning by Monday.

> Friday – Wednesday – Monday – Thursday – Sunday – Tuesday – Saturday

_____, _____, _____, _____,

_____, _____, _____

4 Follow the pattern:

   a) I – going to visit you – Monday – 5

   I am going to visit you on Monday at five.

   b) He – going to visit Mary – Tuesday – 6

   _____

   c) She – going to the party – Wednesday – 7

   _____

   d) You – going to swim – Thursday – 8

   _____

   e) They – going to the movies – Friday – 9

   _____

   f) We – going to dance – Saturday – 10

   _____

5 Complete with the correct preposition:

   a) _____ ten to eight

   b) _____ Saturday

   c) _____ the morning

   d) _____ half past three

   e) _____ the evening

   f) _____ four o'clock

   g) _____ night

   h) _____ Monday

   i) _____ midnight

   j) _____ Sunday

6 Write after or before in the blank spaces. Follow the example:

   Sunday Sunday comes after Saturday and before Monday.

   a) Wednesday   Wednesday comes _____ Tuesday and _____ Thursday.

   b) Saturday   Saturday comes _____ Friday and _____ Sunday.

   c) Tuesday   Tuesday comes _____ Monday and _____ Wednesday.

   d) Friday   Friday comes _____ Thursday and _____ Saturday.

An invitation

Betty: Hello, Simone! I want to invite you to a party on Friday. Are you free on Friday evening?

Simone: I'm sorry, Betty. I'm not free on Friday.

Betty: Why not, Simone?

Simone: On Friday evening I go to the dentist's. But... what kind of party is it?

Betty: It's my birthday party.

Simone: Oh, really? Great! Then I'm going to visit you on Saturday evening. I have some good news for you. Wait for me. Bye, and happy birthday!

Betty: Thanks! Bye! See you on Saturday!

TEXT COMPREHENSION

1. Who is inviting Simone to a party?

2. When is the party?

3. Is Simone free on Friday?

4. Where is Simone going on Friday?

5 What is Simone going to do next week?
Look at Simone's Diary and answer.

Simone's diary

On Monday
Help Paul: 8 a.m.

On Tuesday
Swim at the Club
6 p.m.

On Wednesday
Clean the House

On Thursday
Movies with Jim:
8 p.m.

On Friday
Dentist's
7 p.m.

On Saturday
Meet Betty: 9 p.m.

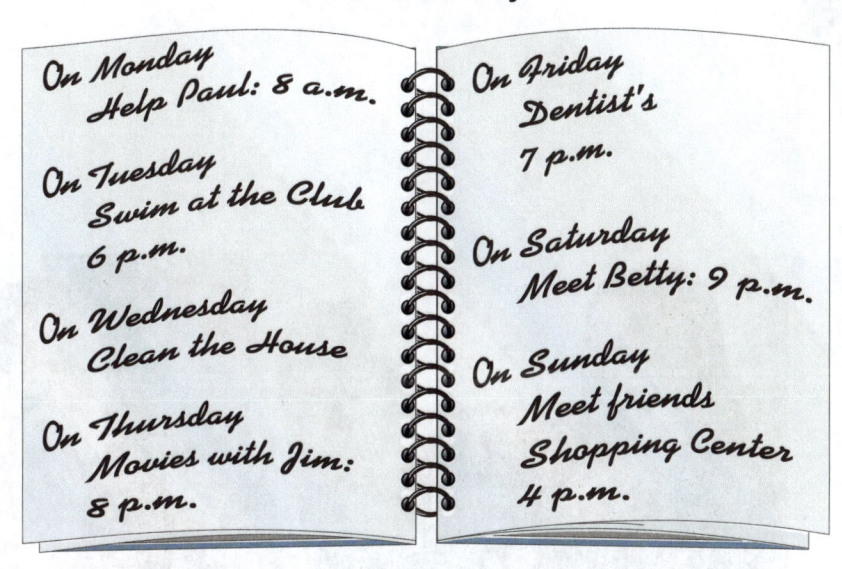

On Sunday
Meet friends
Shopping Center
4 p.m.

Look at Simone's Diary and write what she is going to do in the week.

a) On Monday Simone is going to help Paul at eight a.m.

b) On Tuesday _____

c) _____

d) _____

e) _____

f) _____

g) _____

Now it's your turn

Based on Simone's diary, write in the diary below what you are going to do next week.

My Diary for the next week

On Monday _____
On Tuesday _____
On Wednesday _____
On Thursday _____
On Friday _____
On Saturday _____
On Sunday _____

Lesson 8
SEASONS AND WEATHER

I prefer summer time

Julie: Hello, Liz!
Liz: Hello, Julie!
Julie: Can you come to my house tomorrow? It is my birthday!
Liz: Oh, happy birthday Julie! But I'm sorry, I can't go.
Julie: Why?
Liz: Because I'm going to travel tomorrow.
Julie: And where are you going to?
Liz: I'm going to visit my aunt in Argentina.
Julie: It's very cold there now. It's winter time. I hate winter! I prefer summer time, sun and sea... It's so nice! Oh, Liz, have a good trip!
Liz: Thank you, Julie. Once more, happy birthday! I'm going to send you some postcards from Argentina. Goodbye!
Julie: Goodbye! Have a good time!

TEXT COMPREHENSION

Answer according to the text:

1 Who is inviting Liz to a birthday party?
_____

2 Is Liz sorry or happy because she can't go to Julie's birthday?
_____

3 Why can't Liz go to Julie's birthday?
_____

4 In Argentina the weather is
( ) hot   ( ) warm   ( ) cold   ( ) frozen

5 Who hates cold weather?
_____

6 Liz congratulates to Julie:
( ) on her success in the exams   ( ) on her birthday

7 Julie wishes to her friend Liz:
( ) a happy holiday   ( ) a good trip   ( ) good luck

8 What's the opposite of summer?
_____

9 A relative is
( ) a friend of your family   ( ) a member of your family, like aunt, uncle, cousin...

The weather

There are four seasons in the year:

Seasons
spring – summer – autumn (fall) – winter

Word bank

weather: clima, tempo (meteorológico)

season: estação (do ano)

cold: frio

warm: temperado

cool: agradável

Spring – Spring is the season of flowers. There are green trees and birds singing everywhere. In spring, nature is very beautiful. The weather is warm.

sixty-five **65**

Summer – In summer it is hot. The sun shines brightly. People usually go to the beach or to a swimming pool.

Autumn (fall) – Autumn (or fall) is the season of fruit. The wind blows and the leaves fall from the trees.

Winter – Winter is a cold season. It snows in Europe, in North America and in many other countries. In Brazil, it snows a little in the southern states. In winter, we wear sweaters and coats.

TEXT COMPREHENSION

1 a) What are the seasons of the year?
_____

b) What is the weather like in spring?
_____

c) What is the weather like in summer?
_____

d) What is the weather like in winter?
_____

2 Match the seasons with the words

1. Snow   (   ) Summer

2 . Flowers   (   ) Winter

3. Sunny days   (   ) Fall

4. Fall of the leaves   (   ) Spring

66 sixty-six

LEARN THIS

1. As estações do ano se escrevem com letra inicial minúscula em inglês:
spring, summer, autumn (fall), winter.

2. autumn (inglês britânico)
fall (inglês americano)

3. The weather
Em inglês usamos termos diferentes para designar os diversos graus de temperatura. Veja:

hot: muito quente, calor desconfortável

warm: levemente quente, calor agradável

cool: levemente frio, frio agradável

cold: frio intenso, desconfortável

freezing: gelado

4. Dependendo das estações do ano e de outros fatores, o tempo pode mudar muito. Pode estar:

sunny: ensolarado   **snowy**: com neve
rainy: chuvoso   **steady**: firme
stormy: tempestuoso   **foggy**: com névoa
windy: com ventos   **wet**: úmido
icy: gelado   **dry**: seco
cloudy: nublado

Stormy

Cloudy

Windy

Snowy

sixty-seven 67

ACTIVITIES

1 Write the words hot, warm, cool, cold, freezing according to the thermometers below:

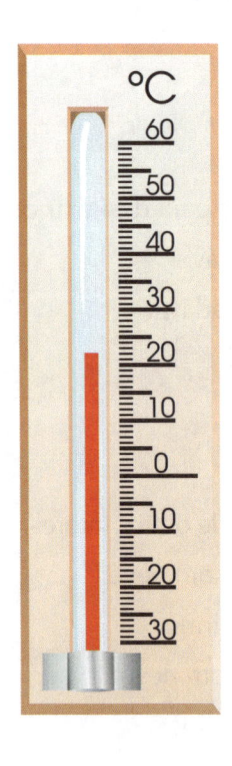

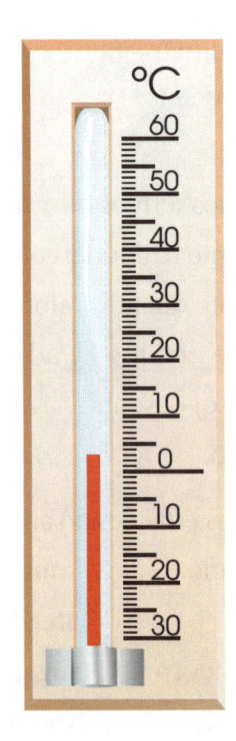

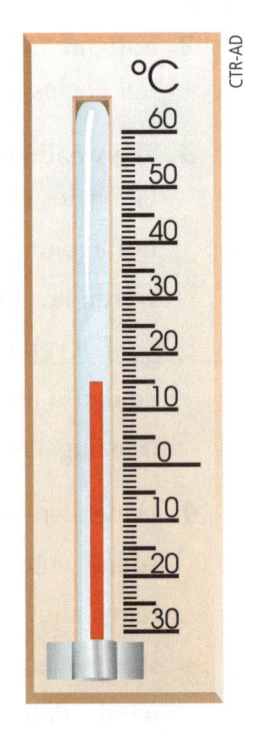

_____   _____   _____   _____   _____

2 Write the appropriate adjectives according to the nouns and the pictures:

clouds: _____   wind: _____   rain: _____

snow: _____   storm: _____   sun: _____

ROLE-PLAY – ORAL DRILL

Weather map

3 Look at the weather map and practice with a classmate about the weather in the capitals of the Brazilian States.

Follow the example:

You: What's the weather like in Recife?

Classmate: It's sunny and hot. The temperature in Recife is thirty degrees.

You: According to the information of the weather map, what's the weather like in Florianópolis?

Classmate: It's cloudy and windy. The temperature in Florianópolis is eighteen degrees.

LET'S SING!

Seasons

I like the sunshine.
I like the moonlight.
And I like the wind
Singing an old song.

Spring is beautiful.
Summer is very sunny.
In fall the wind blows.
In winter it snows.

I like the sunshine.
I like the moonlight.
And I like the wind
Singing an old song.

I like spring,
The season of flowers.
The season of love, too,
for me and you.

Antes de cantar a música, ouça o professor ou o CD, prestando atenção na pronúncia das palavras e procurando saber o significado delas.

Lesson 9

Verb to have; Let's, Let us, too, no

Let's enjoy life!

In summer it is hot and sunny.
People usually go to the beach or to the swimming pool.

Alan: Let's go to the beach, Joe?

Joe: Oh, that's a good idea! We don't have air conditioning in this office. It's impossible to work here today! It's so hot! But look at the sky... I think it's going to rain...

Alan: Oh, no! The sun is shining and there are no clouds in the sky. It's too hot but there is a pleasant breeze coming from the ocean...

Joe: Oh, a pleasant breeze... warm water... a cold juice... ice creams...

Alan: Don't waste your time! Shut the windows and the doors and let's enjoy life!

TEXT COMPREHENSION

1 Who invites Joe to go to the beach?
_____

2 Where are Alan and Joe?
_____

3 According to the text, what is the weather like today?
_____

4 Is there air conditioning in the office?
_____

5 Complete the answer:

Why are Alan and Joe going to the beach?

They are going to the beach because it is impossible _____ in the _____.

It is too _____.

6 Who thinks it's going to rain?

( ) Joe   ( ) Alan

7 Complete: the answer:

Alan thinks it's not going to rain. Why?

Because the sun is _____ and there are no _____ in the sky.

8 The temperature on the beach is

( ) pleasant   ( ) unpleasant

9 Complete: The temperature is pleasant because there is a _____ coming from the ocean.

10 Joe dreams with pleasant things on the beach.

Which are they?

They are: _____ a cold juice and _____

11 According to you, are Joe and Alan responsible people?

(Give a short answer in English and explain your answer in Portuguese.)
_____
_____

seventy-one 71

LEARN THIS

1. Let us and let's

A expressão **let us** ou **let's** (vamos) é usada para se convidar alguém a fazer algo ou apresentar alguma sugestão. **Let's** é a forma contraída de **Let us**.

Let's go to the beach. (Vamos à praia.)

Let's visit Mary. (Vamos visitar Mary.)

2. Affirmative, negative and interrogative forms of the verb to have (simple present)

FULL FORM Affirmative	CONTRACTED FORM Affirmative	FULL FORM Negative	CONTRACTED FORM Negative
I have	I've	I do not have	I don't have
You have	You've	You do not have	You don't have
He has	He's	He does not have	He doesn't have
She has	She's	She does not have	She doesn't have
It has	It's	It does not have	It doesn't have
We have	We've	We do not have	We don't have
You have	You've	You do not have	You don't have
They have	They've	They do not have	They don't have

3. No + substantivo.

O adjetivo indefinido **no** é usado antes do substantivo com sentido negativo e significa: nenhum, nenhuma. Observe que o verbo virá na forma afirmativa.

There are no clouds in the sky.

There is no money in my pocket.

4. Too + adjetivo.

A palavra **too** antes de um adjetivo tem caráter intensificador, significa demais, implica em excesso, exagero.

It's too hot here. (Está muito quente aqui.)

She is too childish. (Ela é infantil demais.)

5. Too no final da frase

Se a palavra **too** vier depois do adjetivo ou no final de frase tem sentido de adição e significa também.

She's beautiful, too (Ela é bonita também.)

In São Paulo it is hot, too. (Em São Paulo está quente também.)

Observação:

O verbo **to have** (ter) pode ser usado como auxiliar ou como verbo principal. Neste último caso, as formas interrogativa e negativa são feitas mediante o emprego do auxiliar **to do**.

ACTIVITIES

1 Make suggestions using let's followed by: eat something / drink an orange juice / go out / take a taxi / watch a TV program / help Roger / play cards / visit uncle John / invite the teachers to a party / walk in the park. Follow the pattern:

a) Let's eat something.

b) _____

c) _____

d) _____

e) _____

f) _____

g) _____

h) _____

2 Translate into Portuguese:

a) These shoes are too big for me.

_____

b) He is my teacher, too.

_____

c) You are too thin! You must eat more!

_____

d) Are you from Italy, too?

_____

3 Fill in the blanks with has or have:

a) I _____ one brother and two sisters.

b) The house _____ three bedrooms.

c) She _____ ten dollars.

d) I _____ no time.

e) Peter _____ many friends.

f) _____ you _____ a good reason to go out?

g) He _____ a place to stay.

4 Translate into Portuguese:

a) There is no water in the vase. _____

b) There are no books on the table. _____

5 Rewrite the words in the correct order and form sentences:

a) sky – clouds – are – there – no – in – the _____

b) hot – coffee – this – is – too _____

c) money – no – have – they _____

_____

FUN TIME

Spot the differences

1 Find out five differences between these pictures and connect the names to the pictures:

cloud   balloon   flag   church   house

2 What's the odd word? Underline it.

a) January, March, June, April, spring, May

b) Sunday, Monday, summer, Friday, Saturday, Tuesday

c) night, morning, evening, month, afternoon

LET'S SING

Friendship

Hi there! Dear friend!
Wait a minute. Come here!
Hi there! Dear friend!
Please come here!
Everything is fine

When we have good friends.
My friends are your friends
And your friends are my friends.
Everything is fine
Because we are good friends.

Antes de cantar a música, ouça o professor ou o CD, prestando atenção na pronúncia das palavras. Procure, também, saber o significado delas.

Vacation in Rio

Karen: Hello, Suzy!
Suzy: Hello, Karen. How are you?
Karen: I'm fine, and you?
Suzy: I'm all right, my dear.
Karen: I want to invite you to spend your vacation with me in Rio.
Suzy: It's a wonderful idea! But is there bedroom for me in your house?
Karen: Yes, there is a comfortable bedroom for you in my house. Can you come?
Suzy: Sure! I can go next week, on Friday.
Karen: I'm waiting for you. Are you coming by bus or by plane?
Suzy: By bus. The 10 o'clock bus in the morning!
Karen: Ok. I'm going to pick you up at the bus station.
Suzy: Karen, thank you for your invitation! You are a really good friend. Goodbye!
Karen: Goodbye!

TEXT COMPREHENSION

Answer according to the text:

1. Who lives in Rio? Karen or Suzy?
   _____

2. How is Karen?
   _____

3. How is Suzy?
   _____

4. Who invites Suzy to spend her vacation in Rio?
   _____

5. Is there a bedroom for Suzy in Karen's house?
   _____

6. Complete?

   Suzy is going to Rio next _____ by _____.

7. Who is going to take Suzy at the bus station?
   _____

8. Is Karen really a good friend?
   _____

After a week

Dear Mom!
I'm writing this postcard from
the Corcovado.
Karen is here with me. We are
enjoying a wonderful view from here.
During the day we go to the beach
and at night we go to the movies and walk
along the beach
                    Love
                              Suzy

TEXT COMPREHENSION

Answer according to the text of the postcard:

1) Where are Suzy and Karen?
_____

2) What's Suzy writing?
_____

3) Suzy is writing a postcard to
   ( ) her friend   ( ) her dad   ( ) her mom

4) Is the view from Corcovado beautiful?
_____

5) What's the girls' vacation like?
_____

6) Write what Suzy and Karen do:

   a) during the day
   _____

   b) at night
   _____

Lesson 10
Past tense of verb to be and verb there to be

In those days...

My name is Ana Frida. I am sixty years old now.
Today, life is very easy but when I was a child it was very difficult. My family was poor and big. I had five sisters and four brothers.
I was up at six o'clock every day.
The school was far from my house and there was no transport, so I had to walk several kilometers to reach school. The teachers were very strict in those days and there were no distractions, but we were happy.

TEXT COMPREHENSION

1
a) What is Ana's surname?
_____

b) Is Ana Frida young or old?
_____

c) How old is Ana Frida?
_____

d) Was life easy or difficult when Ana Frida was a child?
_____

e) Is life easy today?
_____

f) Was Ana's family rich or poor?
_____

g) How many brothers and sisters were there in Ana's family?
_____

h) Was Ana's school near or far from her house?
_____

2 Choose the correct alternative:

a) Ana Frida belongs to
   ( ) a small family.
   ( ) a big family.

b) In those days
   ( ) there was a lot of transport.
   ( ) there was no transport.

c) In those days
   ( ) the teachers were very strict.
   ( ) the teachers were very kind.

d) In those days
   ( ) there were many distractions.
   ( ) there were no distractions.

LEARN THIS

1.

Verb to be Past tense Affirmative form	Verb to be Past tense Negative form	Verb to be Past tense Negative contracted form	Verb to be Past tense Interrogative form
I was	I was not	I wasn't	Was I ?
You were	You were not	You weren't	Were you?
He was	He was not	He wasn't	Was he?
She was	She was not	She wasn't	Was she ?
It was	It was not	It wasn't	Was it ?
We were	We were not	We weren't	Were we?
You were	You were not	You weren't	Were you ?
They were	They were not	They weren't	Were they?

You were (vocês eram, vocês foram/vocês estiveram, vocês estavam)

They were (eles/elas eram, eles/elas foram/eles/elas estiveram, eles/elas estavam)

2. When = quando – **I was very glad when he was at home**.

3. Verb there to be (verbo haver)

Past tense

Affirmative form

There was: havia (singular)

There were: havia (plural)

Interrogative form

Was there...?: havia...? (singular)

Were there...?: havia...? (plural)

Negative form

There was not/There wasn't: não havia (singular)

There were not/There weren't: não havia (plural)

Example: Affirm. **There was a boy in the class**. (Havia um menino na classe.)
Interr. **Was there a boy in the class**? (Havia um menino na classe?)
Negat. **There was not a boy in the class**. (Não havia um menino na classe.)
Affirm. **There were boys in the class**. (Havia meninos na classe.)
Interr. **Were there boys in the class**? (Havia meninos na classe?)
Negat. **There were not boys in the class**. (Não havia meninos na classe.)

seventy-nine **79**

ACTIVITIES

1 Fill in the blanks with there was or there were:

a) _____ a garden in front of the house.

b) _____ strict teachers in my school.

c) _____ beautiful girls at the party.

d) _____ few boys in my class.

e) _____ a good reason to go home.

2 Follow the pattern:

a) (I – young / Now – old)   **I was young. Now I am old.**

b) (I – poor / Now – rich)   _____

c) (I – lazy / Now – hardworking)   _____

d) (The box – full / Now – empty)   _____

e) (You – right / Now – wrong)   _____

3 Rewrite the sentences in the interrogative and negative form:

a) There was a TV in the hotel.

_____

_____

b) There were mistakes in the test.

_____

_____

4 Fill in the blanks with the verb to be in the past tense:

An exciting soccer match

Yesterday _____ a special day for my team. It _____ the final of the Brazilian Football Cup. The match _____ at the Morumbi Stadium in São Paulo. The stadium _____ completely full of supporters. The two finalist teams _____ Corinthians and Flamengo. The match _____ on TV at four o'clock. I _____ very anxious at my friend's house. The players _____ very nervous. The match _____ excellent. Finally just in the last minute my team scored a marvelous goal.

5 Complete the table with the verb **to be** in the past tense:

	affirmative	negative
I – he – she – it	was	_____ / _____
we – you – they	_____	were not / weren't

6 Complete the sentence with was or were:

Jane: What day _____ yesterday?

Jim: Yesterday _____ Friday.

Jane: Where _____ you?

Jim: I _____ at the club, playing football.

Jane: _____ your friends James and Albert with you?

Jim: No, they _____ not. They _____ at the movies.

7 Complete with is, was, are, were:

a) Who _____ absent yesterday?

b) Where _____ you last night?

c) Mary is here now but last year she _____ in France.

d) She _____ very slim now, but she _____ very fat a year ago.

e) – Where _____ you from?
   – I am from Goiânia.

8 Make the question and answer. Follow the pattern:

a) (your sister – seventeen)   **How old is your sister?**
My sister is seventeen years old.

b) (your father – forty) _____

c) (your mother – thirty-five) _____

9 Follow the pattern:

a) (Brazil – Japan)   **Brazil is far from Japan.**

b) (Rio – Paris) _____

c) (Argentina – Canada) _____

d) (The Sun – the Earth) _____

Lesson 11

INTERROGATIVE WORDS

In a job agency

Roberto: Good morning.

Job agency: Good morning.

Roberto: Is there a job for me in your agency?

Job agency: Yes, there is, but first of all, let's sit down to fill out a form.

Job agency: What's your name?

Roberto: My name is Roberto Gouveia.

Job agency: Where are you from?

Roberto: I am from Minas but now I live in São Paulo.

Job agency: What is your address?

Roberto: I live at 22 Pintassilgo Street.

Job agency: What's your telephone number?

Roberto: My telephone number is 55507475.

Job agency: When were your born?

Roberto: I was born on May 24th, 1995.

Job agency: What was your last job?

Roberto: I was an office boy in a shopping center.

Job agency: I think I have a job for you in a restaurant.

Roberto: What kind of job is it?

Job agency: Pizza deliverer.

Roberto: How much is the pay?

Job agency: Seven hundred and forty reais.

Roberto: That's fine, but where is the restaurant? What's its name?

Job agency: It's the Italian Pizza Restaurant on Rome Street.

Roberto: When may I begin work?

Job agency: Tomorrow from 7 p.m. to midnight.

Roberto: Thank you very much.

TEXT COMPREHENSION

1 The interview in the job agency is
   ( ) in the morning
   ( ) in the afternoon
   ( ) in the evening
   ( ) at night

2 What is Roberto's surname?

_____

3 Complete:

Roberto _____ but he lives _____

4 What is Roberto's address?

_____

5 What is his telephone number?
_____

6 When was Roberto born?
_____

7 What was Roberto's last job?
_____

8 Roberto is going to work in a(an)
( ) Chinese restaurant
( ) Italian restaurant
( ) Greek restaurant

9 What is the name of the restaurant?
_____

10 Roberto is going to work in the Italian Pizza Restaurant
( ) during the day   ( ) during the night

11 Where is the Italian Pizza Restaurant?
_____

12 How much is Roberto going to receive as a pizza deliverer?
_____

LEARN THIS

Interrogative words

1. **Who?** (Quem?) Usa-se para pessoas:
   - **Who are you?** (Quem é você?)
   - **I'm Roberto.** (Sou Roberto.)
   - **Who are those people?** (Quem são aquelas pessoas?)
   - **They are Jane and Mark**. (São Jane e Mark.)

2. **What?** (Quê?/Qual?/O quê?/Quais?)
   What is this? (O que é isto?)
   What is your name? (Qual é o seu nome?)
   What do you do? (O que você faz? Qual é a sua ocupação?)
   What time is it? (Que horas são?)
   What is happening? (O que está acontecendo?)
   What is the color of the sky? (Qual é a cor do céu?)
   What are the colors of the flag? (Quais são as cores da bandeira?)
   What is the matter? (Qual é o problema?)

3. **How?** (Como?/De que modo?)
   How are you? (Como vai você?)
   How old are you? (Qual é a sua idade?)
   How many books? (Quantos livros?)
   How lovely this is! (Que bonito é!)

4. **Where?** (Onde?)
   Where are you? (Onde está você?)
   Where are they? (Onde estão eles?)
   Where is my book? (Onde está meu livro?)
   Where is the post office? (Onde fica o correio?)
   Where are you going? (Para onde você vai?)

5. **When?** (Quando?)
   When were you in Brasília? (Quando você esteve em Brasília?)
   When are you going? (Quando você vai?)
   When is your birthday? (Quando é seu aniversário?)

6. **Why?** (Por quê?)
   Why are you happy? (Por que você está feliz?)
   Why are they late? (Por que eles estão atrasados?)
   Why not? (Por que não?)
   Why are you crying? (Por que você está chorando?)

ACTIVITIES

1 Follow the pattern:
Use is or are:

a) **Who – that boy? – Peter**
   Who is that boy?
   He is Peter. (ou respondendo com o pronome neutro: **It's Peter.**)

b) Who – that girl? – Mary

_____

_____

c) Who – those boys? – John and Anthony

_____

_____

d) Who – these people? – Jane, Michael, Bob

e) Who – you? – Paul

f) Who – he? – Thomas

g) Who – they? – Daniel, Diana

2 Write in English:

a) Qual é o seu nome?

b) Qual é a sua profissão?

c) O que é isto?

d) O que é aquilo?

e) De onde você é?

f) Qual é o problema?

g) Quais são as cores da bandeira brasileira?

h) Que horas são?

i) Qual é o seu endereço?

j) O que você faz?
___

k) Como vai você?
___

l) Qual é a sua idade?
___

m) Onde estão meus livros?
___

n) Quando é seu aniversário?
___

o) Onde você está?
___

3 Ask questions for these answers. Use the interrogative words in the box:

| How old | When | How | Why | What time |
| Where | What | Who | What color | |

a) ___
My name is John Addams.

b) ___
My mother's name is Mariana.

c) ___
I am from Bahia.

d) ___
My telephone number is 55555459.

e) ___
Her birthday is on June, 7th.

f) ___
She was born on July 27th, 1980.

g) ___
I am fourteen years old.

h) ___
I am well, thanks.

eighty-seven **87**

Lesson 12

PLURAL OF NOUNS

Fair on Sampson Street

Mom: Jenny, are you ready?
Jenny: Where are we going?
Mom: To the fair on Sampson Street.
Jenny: Ok, mom. Let's go.

Jenny: Mom, let's go to a supermarket. The fair is crowded. We can't walk calmly with the carts, dogs, men, women and children on the street!
Mom: I prefer the fair. At the fair the fruit and vegetables are fresh and cheap.

At the tomatoes stand

Mom: How much is one kilo of these tomatoes?
Mr Ellis: It costs two dollars.
Mom: It's too expensive.
Mr Ellis: I can give you a 50 percent discount.
Mom: Thank you. Here you are.
Mr Ellis: Thank you and come back soon.

At the fruit stand

Mom: How much is a kilo of these papayas?
Mr Green: It's one dollar and fifty cents.
Mom: That's OK. Take two dollars.
Mr Green: Here are your papaya and change.
Mom: Thank you, Mr Green.

TEXT COMPREHENSION

1 Where are Jenny and mom going?
_____

2 Where is the fair?
_____

3 Who wants to go to the fair? Why?
_____
_____

5 What is the opposite of cheap?
_____

6 How much is a kilo of tomatoes?
_____

7 How much is a kilo of papaya?
_____

LEARN THIS

PLURAL OF NOUNS

1. Regra geral; geralmente forma-se o plural dos substantivos acrescentando-se **s** ao singular:

street – streets   **dollar – dollars**   **dog – dogs**

2. Os substantivos terminados em **y** precedido de vogal seguem a regra geral: acrescenta-se **s** ao singular:

boy – boys   **key – keys**   **toy – toys**   **day – days**

3. Os substantivos terminados em **y** precedido de consoante formam o plural trocando o **y** por **ies**:

lady – ladies   **secretary – secretaries**   **city – cities**
family – families   **candy – candies**   **baby – babies**

4. Os substantivos terminados por **man** no singular formam o plural trocando-se o **man** por **men**:

man – men   **mailman – mailmen**   **woman – women**
postman – postmen   **policeman – policemen**   **gentleman – gentlemen**

5. Nos substantivos terminados em **s**, **sh**, **ch**, **x**, **z**, **o** geralmente acrescenta-se **es** para se formar o plural:

bus – buses   beach – beaches   fox – foxes   hero – heroes
glass – glasses   watch – watches   box – boxes   tomato – tomatoes
ash – ashes   peach – peaches   tax – taxes   echo – echoes
flash – flashes   church – churches

6. Irregular plurals – Os plurais irregulares não seguem as regras anteriores.
Lista de alguns plurais irregulares:

Singular	Plural
child (criança)	children (crianças)
man (homem)	men (homens)
woman (mulher)	women (mulheres)
goose (ganso)	geese (gansos)
mouse (camundongo)	mice (camundongos)
louse (piolho)	lice (piolhos)
ox (boi)	oxen (bois)
foot (pé)	feet (pés)
tooth (dente)	teeth (dentes)

7. A palavra **people** significa pessoas, gente, e leva o verbo para o plural:
They are good people. (Eles são boas pessoas.)

8. Prepositions of place: **on**, **at**
a) Quando, na frase, aparece apenas o nome da rua, sem citar o número, usa-se a preposição **on**:
She lives on Sampson Street. (Ela mora na rua Sampson.)
I live on Paulista Avenue.
b) Porém, se além do nome da rua aparece o número, usa-se a preposição **at**:
They live at 27 California Street. (Eles moram na rua Califórnia número 27.)
I live at 51 East Side Street.
c) Usamos a preposição **on** antes de **farm** (fazenda). **The Smiths live on a farm near Cuiabá**.

ACTIVITIES

1 Follow the pattern:

a) 1 boy / 4... **One boy / four boys**

b) 1 day / 3... _____

c) 1 key / 5... _____

d) 1 play / 6... _____

e) 1 monkey / 8... _____

f) 1 donkey / 9... _____

g) 1 toy / 7... _____

2 Follow the pattern:

a) 1 city / 3... One city / three cities

b) 1 candy / 7... _____

c) 1 lady / 10... _____

d) 1 family / 5... _____

e) 1 quality / 2... _____

f) 1 activity / 4... _____

g) 1 secretary / 9... _____

3 Write in the plural:

a) The tomato is in the box.
_____

b) There is a yellow peach in the basket.
_____

c) The lady is near the child.
_____

d) I've got a good watch.
_____

4 Write in English:

a) Há homens e mulheres na feira.   _____

b) Os legumes estão frescos e baratos.   _____

c) Há tomates e batatas dentro das caixas. _____

5 Change the sentences to the plural form:

a) There is a boy in the class.
_____

b) Is your child well?
_____

c) Is the beach dirty?
_____

d) His country is now independent.
_____

6 Complete the sentences with the prepositions in, at or on:

a) The peaches are _____ the box.

b) We live _____ Colorado Street.

c) The books are _____ the table.

d) My cousin lives _____ Porto Alegre.

e) The post office is _____ 29 Porto Rico Street.

f) They work _____ a shop _____ Virginia Street.

FUN TIME

A plural crossword puzzle

1 Complete the crossword puzzle according to the pictures:

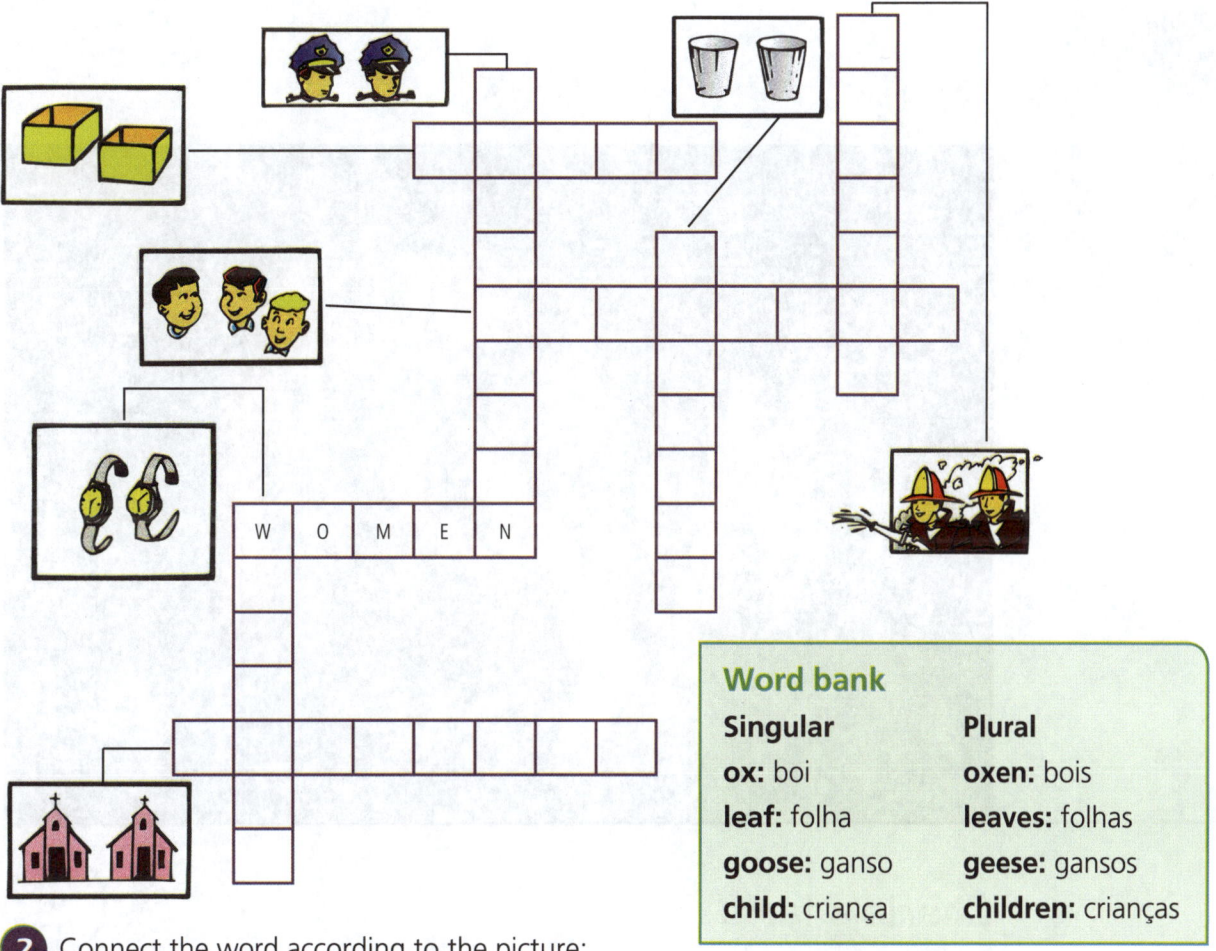

W O M E N

Word bank

Singular	Plural
ox: boi	**oxen:** bois
leaf: folha	**leaves:** folhas
goose: ganso	**geese:** gansos
child: criança	**children:** crianças

2 Connect the word according to the picture:

children
leaves
geese
tomatoes
oxen
ladies
men
man
beaches
foxes

ninety-three **93**

Lesson 13

PLURAL OF NOUNS

Charle's farm

Charles has got a large farm. Many people work there. Men and women work daily in all sorts of jobs. Charles milks his cows every day.

There are big animals on the farm, like cows, oxen, horses and small animals like hens, geese and pigs. Charles has got many buffaloes and sheep. He is a rich farmer.

There are also five large lakes on the farm with tons of fish. And there is a beautiful orchard with many kinds of fruit.

And people on the farm don't pollute nature. They live in a healthy environment.

It is really a very nice farm.

TEXT COMPREHENSION

1
a) Is Charles' farm large or small?
_____

b) Who works on Charles' farm?
_____

c) Name some big animals on Charles' farm.
_____

d) Is Charles lazy or hardworking?
_____

e) How many lakes are there on Charles' farm?
_____

2 Write **true** or **false** according to the text:

(_____) Charles has got a large and nice farm.

(_____) Many people work on Charles' farm.

(_____) Only men work on Charles' farm.

LEARN THIS

PLURAL OF NOUNS

1. Nas palavras a seguir, os dois **oo** são substituídos por dois **ee** no plural:

goose – geese (ganso – gansos)

foot – feet (pé – pés)

tooth – teeth (dente – dentes)

2. Plural of nouns ending in "j" or "fe":

As palavras terminadas em **f** (ou **fe**) no singular geralmente mudam o **f** (ou **fe**) por **v** no plural e recebem **es**:

bookshelf – bookshelves (estante – estantes)

leaf – leaves (folha – folhas)

wolf – wolves (lobo – lobos)

life – lives (vida – vidas)

knife – knives (faca – facas)

wife – wives (esposa – esposas)

3. Alguns substantivos têm a mesma forma para o singular e para o plural:

fish (peixe – peixes)*

sheep (ovelha – ovelhas)

fruit (fruta – frutas)

4. A palavra **news** (novidade, notícia) só é empregada no singular:

What is the news? (Quais são as novidades?)

This news is fantastic! (Esta notícia é fantástica!)

*Obs.: usa-se **fishes** e **fruits** quando se trata de espécies e variedades.

ACTIVITIES

1 Write in the plural:

(Note that the article a/an disappears in the plural. Pay attention to the verbal forms: singular – is, was; plural – are, were.)

a) There is a goose in the lake.

b) There was an ox in the field.

c) A leaf is falling from the tree.

d) He works for a large factory.

e) There was a bus in the park.

f) There is a mouse near the house.

g) There is a sheep in the field.

h) There was a fox in the forest.

2 Write in the plural:

a) a white tooth

b) a wild wolf

c) a green leaf

d) a nice lady

e) a lovely baby

3 Change to the singular form:

a) There were children in the cars.

b) There are geese in those lakes.

c) They have got white knives.

d) We are taking buses.

FUN TIME

1 Translate.

1. Ovos
2. Cidades
3. Pessoas
4. Fruta ou frutas
5. Pés
6. Ratos
7. Homens
8. Novidade ou novidades
9. Peixe ou peixes
10. Bois
11. Igrejas
12. Gansos
13. Dentes

2 Complete the crossword puzzle.

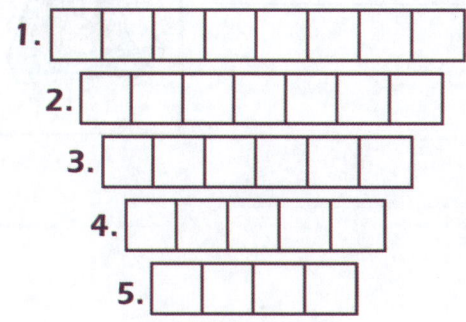

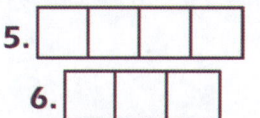

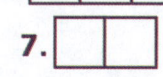

ninety-seven 97

1.
2.
3.
4.
5.
6.
7.

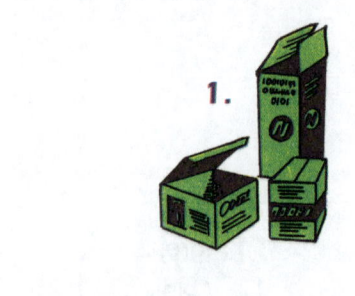

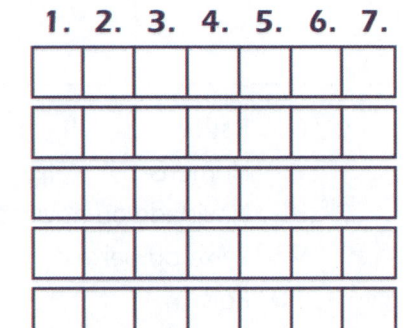

3 Look at the model and do the same.

books on the table
How many books are there on the table?
There are two books on the table.

lamps in the room
_____
_____
_____
_____

cars in front of the house
_____
_____
_____
_____

oranges in the box
_____
_____
_____
_____

98 ninety-eight

Lesson 14

PREPOSITIONS

The living room

Look at the living room of my house. It is large and comfortable. Tom, my dad is sitting on his favorite armchair. He is reading a newspaper. Emilie, my sister, is watching TV on a sofa. My dog is in front of the door.

What can you see on the left of the living room?

I can see a _____
_____

What can you see in the center of the living room?

I can see a table, _____
_____

What can you see on the right of the living room?

I can see _____

TEXT COMPREHENSION

1 Answer according to the text:

a) Who is the man in the living room?
_____

b) What is he reading?
_____

c) Who is the girl in the living room?
_____

d) What is she doing?
_____

e) Where is she sitting?
_____

2 Look at the picture of the living room and answer the questions:

a) Is the girl on the right or on the left of the living room?
_____

b) Is the bookcase near or far from the girl?
_____

c) Are there many books in the bookcase?
_____

d) Where is the radio?
_____

e) Where is the lamp?
_____

f) Where is the girl sitting?
_____

3 Look at the center of the picture and choose the correct alternative:

a) The man in the center of the living room is reading
( ) a book   ( ) a newspaper   ( ) a magazine

b) The man is sitting
( ) on a bench   ( ) on a sofa   ( ) on an armchair

c) The small table is
( ) in front of the man   ( ) behind the man

d) The basket with fruit is
( ) under the small table   ( ) on the small table

e) The flower pot and the picture of a baby are
( ) on the bookcase   ( ) on the shelf   ( ) on the small table

4 Look at the left side of the living room and answer the question writing true or false:

a) There is a small dog in the living room.
Where is it?

(_____) It is on the sofa.

(_____) It is between the table and the door.

100 one hundred

b) (_____) The television set is in front of the window.

(_____) The video recorder is under the television set.

c) (_____) The dog is playing with a ball.

(_____) The dog is playing with a cat.

d) (_____) The window is near the television set.

(_____) The window is far from the television set.

LEARN THIS

Prepositions

1. **From** (de)
   From indica origem, procedência, começo:
   From the window of the living room I can see a garden.
   (Da janela da sala de estar eu posso ver um jardim.)
   I come from Rio. (Eu venho do Rio).

2. **To** (para)
   To indica destino, finalidade:
   I go to Rio. (Eu vou para o Rio.)
   Look at the picture. (Olhe para a figura.)

3. **For** (para, por)
   For indica finalidade; duração de tempo:
   Don't sit near the TV, it's bad for you.
   (Não se sente perto da TV, é ruim para você.)
   Stay here for five minutes. (Fique aqui por cinco minutos.)

4. **Between:** (entre dois seres ou dois grupos de seres).
   I am between Mary and John. (Estou entre Mary e John.)

5. **Among** (entre, no meio de muitos)
   I am among friends. (Eu estou entre amigos.)

6. **With** (com)
   I go with you. (Eu vou com você.)

7. **Without** (sem)
   Don't go out without money. (Não saia sem dinheiro.)
   Nota: Observe a posição da preposição **from** na pergunta:
   Where are you from? (De onde você é?)

8. **In front of** (em frente de; na frente de)
   I'm sitting in front of you. (Estou sentado na sua frente.)

9. **Behind** (atrás)
   The yard is behind the house. (O quintal fica atrás da casa.)

ACTIVITIES

1 Look at the pictures and fill in the blanks with the prepositions between, among, with, to, from:

a) Lucy is sitting _____ John and Paul.

b) The woman is _____ the people.

c) The child cuts the finger _____ a knife.

d) The bus is going _____ Rio.

e) The truck is coming _____ Rio.

2 Fill in the blanks with the prepositions from, to, for, between, among, with, without:

a) – Where are you coming _____? – I'm coming _____ Rio.

b) – Where are you going? – I'm going _____ São Paulo.

c) I was at home _____ my mother.

d) The teacher treats all the students _____ distinction.

e) It's about 400 (four hundred) kilometers _____ São Paulo _____ Rio.

REVIEW

Write in the plural:

1 **General rule** ⟶ **– s**
(regra geral: acrescenta-se **s**)

a) friend _____

b) week _____

c) driver _____

d) door _____

2 **Vowel -y** ⟶ **-ys**
(**y** precedido de vogal, acrescenta-se **ys**)

a) toy _____

b) key _____

c) boy _____

d) day _____

3 Consonant -y ⟶ -ies

(**y** precedido de consoante, acrescenta-se **ies**)

a) activity _____
b) city _____
c) lady _____
d) baby _____
e) secretary _____
f) candy _____
g) country _____

4 Irregular plurals -man ⟶ -men

a) man _____
b) woman _____
c) policeman _____
d) mailman _____
e) postman _____
f) gentleman _____

5 Nomes terminados em **-s**, **-sh**, **-ch**, **-x**, **-z**, **-o** ⟶ **-es**

a) fox _____
b) bus _____
c) flash _____
d) church _____
e) potato _____
f) echo _____
g) box _____
h) glass _____
i) beach _____
j) watch _____
k) tomato _____
l) hero _____

6 Irregular plurals oo ⟶ ee

a) goose _____
b) tooth _____
c) foot _____

7 -f, -fe ⟶ ves

a) wife _____
b) knife _____
c) life _____
d) wolf _____
e) leaf _____

8 Write in English:

a) As crianças estão aqui.

_____

b) Há ratos nesta velha casa.

_____

FUN TIME

1 Complete the crossword and find the hidden word:

1. a respeito de, sobre
2. gansos
3. batatas
4. relógio
5. ovelha
6. pés
7. dedo

Hidden word ↓

What's the hidden word? It's _____

LET'S SING

A film on TV

I was at home
Watching a film on TV
It wasn't a horror film
It wasn't a film of war
People in the film
Were dancing and singing

Let's put an end to war
Live and let live
It was a great film
Because it showed peace
It was a wonderful film
Because it showed love

Antes de cantar a música, ouça o professor ou o CD, prestando atenção na pronúncia das palavras. Procure, também, saber o significado delas.

Lesson 15

GENITIVE CASE

Is it good to live in an apartment?

Boy: Is it good to live in an apartment?
Old man: Oh, no! I have great problems with my neighbours.
Boy: What problems?
Old man: The major problem is that it's impossible to sleep well here. In the apartment above, Mary's husband speaks loud and shouts every night.
In the apartment below, John's wife plays the piano and sings loud.
In the apartment on the right, the child's dog barks all night.
In the apartment on the left, Betty's CD player is always too loud.
I'm almost deaf! My neighbours are too noisy.

TEXT COMPREHENSION

1 a) The text is about

( ) life in a house ( ) life in an apartment

b) Who talks to an old man?

_____

c) The old man

( ) lives alone in a house ( ) lives in a flat

d) The old man's neighbours are

( ) good neighbours ( ) noisy neighbours

e) According to the text, what is the major problem to live in an apartment?

_____

f) What is the problem with the apartment above the old man's apartment?

_____

g) What is the problem with the apartment below?

_____

h) What is the problem with the apartment on the right?

_____

i) What is the problem with the apartment on the left?

_____

2 Write (true) or (false):

a) It's good to live in an apartment. (_____)

b) John's wife sings loud. (_____)

c) In the apartment on the left the dog barks. (_____)

d) The old man sleeps well. (_____)

e) There is a dog in the apartment on the right. (_____)

f) Betty lives in the apartment on the left. (_____)

g) Betty is John's wife. (_____)

h) Mary's husband shouts at night. (_____)

LEARN THIS

1. Genitive case

Observe:

Jane's dog. (O cachorro de Jane.)

- no caso genitivo o possuidor vem antes da coisa possuída;
- o possuidor é acompanhado de **'s**;
- o possuidor será acompanhado de um apóstrofo apenas se terminar por **s**. Veja:

My parents' car. (O carro de meus pais.)

Com nomes no singular terminados em **s**, podemos colocar **'s** ou apenas **'**. Observe:

Denis's house./Denis' house. (Casa de Denis.)

Nota importante: geralmente só se usa o caso genitivo (**'s**), (**'**) quando o possuidor é representado por uma pessoa. Com coisas usa-se a preposição **of**:

The branch of the tree. (O galho da árvore.)

The clock of the church. (O relógio da igreja.)

2. Prepositions of place

above: acima

below: abaixo

on the right: à direita

on the left: à esquerda

Examples:
I can see a truck on the right side of the street.
I live in the flat above Mary's.
The Johnsons live in the flat below.

ACTIVITIES

1 Look at the model and do the same:

(Do not use the article before proper nouns in the genitive case.)

a) o carro de John   John's car

b) a casa de Jane   _____

c) o cachorro do Paul   _____

d) o gato da Sibele   _____

e) a bicicleta do Roberto   _____

Lesson 16

Possessive: his, her

Diana's bedroom

Chris: Mike, this is Diana's bedroom.
Mike: Oh, it is large and comfortable.
Chris: What can you see in her bedroom?
Mike: I can see a bed, a wardrobe, a dressing table and a bedside table.
Chris: Can you see where her watch and bracelet are?
Mike: Her watch and bracelet are on the bedside table.
Chris: And where are her slippers?
Mike: Her slippers are on the floor near her bed.
Chris: Can you discover where her alarm clock is?
Mike: Yes. It is on the dressing table.
Chris: Where is her skirt?
Mike: It is on the bed.
Chris: You are a good observer! Congratulations!

Illustrated vocabulary

Look at the picture of Diana's bedroom and write the names of these objects:

lamp

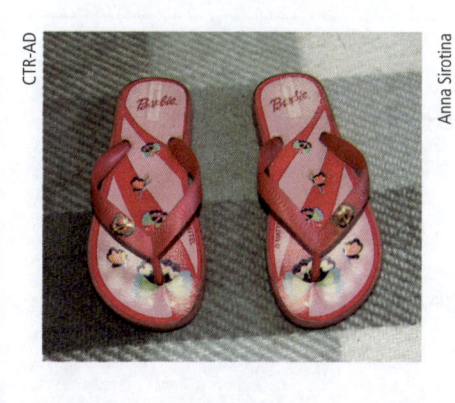

shoes

TEXT COMPREHENSION

Look at the picture of Diana's bedroom and choose the correct alternative:

a) In Diana's bedroom there is

   ( ) a vase with flowers

   ( ) a bed near a bedside table

   ( ) a carpet on the floor

b) On her bedside table

   ( ) there is a bracelet

   ( ) there is a necklace

   ( ) there is a black bag

c) Where is Diana's skirt?

   ( ) Her skirt is on the bed.

   ( ) Her skirt is in the wardrobe.

   ( ) Her skirt is on the floor.

d) Write true or false:

   (_____) Diana's perfume is on the dressing table.

   (_____) Diana's perfume is in her bag.

   (_____) Diana's perfume is in the drawer of the dressing table.

e) Where is Diana's alarm clock?

   ( ) Her alarm clock is in the wardrobe.

   ( ) Her alarm clock is on the bed.

   ( ) Her alarm clock is on the dressing table.

f) Diana's slippers

   ( ) are near her bed

   ( ) are near the wardrobe

REVIEW

1 Look at the model and do the same:
(Do not use the article before proper nouns in the genitive case.)

   a) o carro de John   John's car

   b) a casa de meus pais   _____

c) o galho da árvore _____

d) o gato da Cibele _____

e) a bicicleta de Denis _____

f) o carro de meus amigos _____

2 Follow the pattern:

(Use the article before common nouns in the genitive case.)

a) o livro do professor   **the teacher's book**

b) a casa do dentista _____

c) as canetas do estudante _____

d) a bola do menino _____

e) a boneca da menina _____

3 Follow the pattern:

(Com nomes próprios terminados em **s** podemos optar pelo apóstrofo mais **s** (**'s**) ou simplesmente pelo apóstrofo)

a) carro de Denis
Denis's car/Denis' car

b) a casa de Charles

_____

c) a família de Sócrates

_____

d) o livro de Davis

_____

e) a escola de Moses

_____

4 Follow the pattern:

(When the nouns end with an **s** in the plural, add only an apostrophe)

a) os livros dos estudantes   **the students' books**

b) as revistas das meninas _____

c) os carros dos médicos _____

d) a casa de meus amigos _____

e) as bicicletas dos meninos _____

Jim's bedroom

Tom: Look at Jim's bedroom.
　　　Is it tidy?

Alice: No, his bedroom is a mess!

Tom: Where are his socks?

Alice: His socks are on the floor.

Tom: Where are his tennis shoes?

Alice: They are in the toy box.

Tom: Where are his jeans pants?

Alice: They are under the chair.

Tom: And where is his Teddy bear?
　　　Is it in the box with the other toys?

Alice: No, his Teddy bear is lying on his bed.

Illustrated vocabulary

Look at the picture of Jim's bedroom and write the names of these objects:

_____	_____	**Teddy bear**
_____	_____	**shoes**
_____	_____	_____
_____	_____	_____

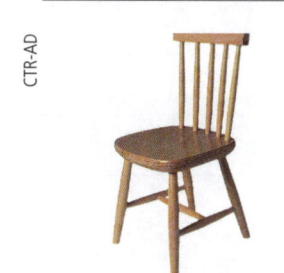

TEXT COMPREHENSION

a) Look at Jim's bed.
   What can you see on his bed?
   I can see:

   ( ) a toy car   ( ) a T-shirt   ( ) a pillow   ( ) a cap

   ( ) a Teddy bear   ( ) a blanket   ( ) an alarm clock   ( ) a ball

b) Where are Jim's toys?

His toys are:

( ) in the toy box   ( ) on the bedside table   ( ) on the bed   ( ) on the floor

c) Put Jim's bedroom in order. Write the name of each object under the correct place:

in the wardrobe	in the toy box	on the desk/ writing-table	on the bedside table
_____	_____	_____	_____
_____	_____	_____	_____
_____	_____	_____	_____
_____	_____	_____	_____
_____	_____	_____	_____
_____	_____	_____	_____
_____	_____	_____	_____
_____	_____	_____	_____

LEARN THIS

1. Possessive: his, her

His (dele, seu, seus, sua, suas)

O possessivo **his** refere-se a um possuidor que é sempre uma pessoa do sexo masculino:

His bedroom is large. (Seu quarto é espaçoso.) (O quarto dele é espaçoso.)

His toys are in the toy box. (Os brinquedos dele estão na caixa de brinquedos.)

Her (dela, seu, seus, sua, suas)

O possessivo **her** refere-se a um possuidor que é sempre uma pessoa do sexo feminino:

Her watch is on the table. (Seu relógio está sobre a mesa.) (O relógio dela está sobre a mesa.)
Her skirt is on the chair. (A saia dela está sobre a cadeira.)

2. Certas palavras da língua inglesa, como **trousers** (calças), **pants** (calças), **scissors** (tesoura), **glasses** (óculos), **jeans** (jeans), **pajamas** (pijamas) são usadas somente na forma plural.

Obs.: **trousers** (British English); **pants** (American English.)

ACTIVITIES

1 Look at the model and do the same:

a) **(house – Mary)**

This house belongs to Mary.

It's Mary's house.

It's her house.

b) (car – Joe)

_____

_____

c) (blouse – Margareth)

_____

_____

_____

d) (bed – Jim)

_____

_____

_____

2 Follow the pattern:

a) **(man – friend – Robert)**

Who's that man?

That man is my friend.

What's his name?

His name is Robert.

b) (boy – brother – Paul)

_____

_____

_____

_____

LET'S SING

My bedroom

My bedroom is always a mess,
but I like my bedroom.
There is a picture on the wall,
It's beautiful and small.

From my bedroom,
on the last floor,
I can see the sky,
I can see the Moon,
I can see the landscape
from my bedroom.
I can see the clouds and the rainbow.

Word bank

bedroom: quarto

always: sempre

mess: bagunça

wall: parede

last floor: último andar

sky: céu

Moon: Lua

landscape: paisagem

clouds: nuvens

rainbow: arco-íris

Antes de cantar a música, ouça o professor ou o CD, prestando atenção na pronúncia das palavras. Procure, também, saber o significado delas.

Lesson 17
POSSESSIVE ADJECTIVES

In a tour agency

Wilson: Good morning

Tour guide: Good morning! Welcome to our agency and to our country – Canada. Where are you from?

Wilson: I'm from Brazil. My name's Wilson Pereira.

Tour guide: Nice to meet you, Mr Wilson Pereira. I like Brazil very much. Can I help you?

Wilson: I want to visit Canada and its attractions. Any suggestions?

Tour guide: Yes! We have many and many suggestions for you. You may visit Toronto, Quebec, Ottawa, Montreal, Niagara Falls, the Rocky Mountains and their attractions. You may know the Canadian people with their traditions, their food, amusements and Canadian natural beauties.

Wilson: Please can I have a booklet and leaflets with photos of cities of Canada?

Tour guide: Sure! Here you are.

Wilson: Thank you!

The Rocky Mountais – Banff (Banff National Park) – Alberta. It is located in Alberta's Rocky Mountains along the Trans-Canada Highway. Banff is a resort town and one of Canada's most popular destinations, known for its hot springs and outdoor aports.

Upper Canada Village, where people live as they were in the XVIII century

Indian Totems near Capilano Bridge – Vancouver. Copilano suspension Bridge is one of the most popular tourist attractions in Vancouver, British Columbia. Totem poles are on display in the Totem Park.

one hundred and seventeen 117

A rotative restaurant in CN Tower, with 553m high – Toronto – Ontario.
The CN Tower is a communication and observation tower. It's the famous symbol of Canada attracting more than two million visitors annually.

Wilson: Oh! Canada is marvelous!

TEXT COMPREHENSION

Answer according to the text:

1. What's the tourist's name? _____
2. Who welcomes Mr Pereira? _____
3. Who's visiting Canada? _____
4. Where is Mr Pereira from? _____
5. What are the tour guide suggestions? _____
_____

6. Mr Pereira has

   ( ) a good impression about Canada

   ( ) a bad impression about Canada

LEARN THIS

1. Possessive adjectives

Personal pronouns		Possessive adjectives
I	→	My (meu, minha, meus, minhas)
You	→	Your (seu, sua, seus, suas, teu, tua…)
He	→	His (dele, seu, sua, seus, suas)
She	→	Her (dela, seu, sua, seus, suas)
It	→	Its (dele, dela, seu, sua, seus, suas)
We	→	Our (nosso, nossa, nossos, nossas)
You	→	Your (seu, sua, seus, suas, vosso, vossa…)
They	→	Their (deles, delas, seu, sua, seus, suas)

2. O verbo **may** é usado com frequência para se pedir licença com formalidade.

   May I come in? (Posso entrar?)

   May I go now? (Posso ir agora?)

3. A palavra **parents** significa pais (**mother and father**). Quando queremos dizer parentes usamos, em inglês, a palavra **relatives** (**uncle**, **aunt**, **cousin**, **nephew**, **niece** etc.)

4. Observe o emprego da preposição **at** nas frases a seguir:

   They are at home. (Eles estão em casa.)

   They are at the table. (Eles estão à mesa.)

   They are at school. (Eles estão na escola.)

   I was there at night. (Eu estive lá à noite.)

   My class begins at 8 o'clock. (Minha aula começa às 8 horas.)

ACTIVITIES

1 Follow the pattern:

   a) (house – blue)
   What color is your house?
   Our house is blue.

   b) (car – black)　　　　　　　　　　c) (ball – red)

   _____　　_____

   _____　　_____

2 Follow the pattern:

   a) His pullover is red. Her pullover is red, too.
   Their pullovers are red.

   b) His house is small. Her house is small, too. _____

   c) His car is new. Her car is new, too. _____

   d) His child is nice. Her child is nice, too. _____

   e) His teacher is good. Her teacher is good, too. _____

   f) His father is old. Her father is old, too. _____

3 Use **his**, **her** or **their**:

   a) This house belongs to John.
   It's his house.

   b) This car belongs to Mary. _____

   c) This bookshop belongs to Margareth. _____

   d) This market belongs to Bob and Larry. _____

   e) This building belongs to Ronald. _____

4 Change to the plural form:

   a) His house is new.　　　　　　　　d) My pencil is black.

   _____　　_____

   b) His car is red.　　　　　　　　　　e) Your shirt is white.

   _____　　_____

   c) Her house is modern.　　　　　　f) My car is old.

   _____　　_____

5 Write his or her:

a) This is Anna's brother. _____

b) That is Adam's sister. _____

c) This book belongs to John. _____

d) That magazine belongs to Linda. _____

e) These skirts belong to Laura. _____

f) Those hats belong to the cowboy. _____

2 Write my or their:

a) This book belongs to me. _____

b) Those bicycles belong to my brothers. _____

c) That car belongs to me. _____

3 Write in English:

a) A blusa de Maria está suja. _____

b) A saia de Diana está limpa. _____

c) O quarto de Charles é pequeno. _____

d) O apartamento de James é novo. _____

e) O marido de Laura é jovem. _____

f) Os sapatos de Roberto estão limpos. _____

g) O vizinho de Adam é um professor. _____

4 Write in English:

a) Elas estavam em casa. _____

b) Os meninos estão à mesa. _____

c) Minha aula começa às sete horas. _____

d) Meus pais e meus parentes estão em casa. _____

5 Follow the pattern:

a) **Ann / hair / black / Mary / blond**

   Ann's hair is black.

   Mary's hair is blond.

b) Peter / car / new / John / old

   _____

   _____

c) Robert / house / small / Adam / large

   _____

   _____

d) Jim / father / old / Bob / young

   _____

   _____

e) Charles / shoes / dirty / Tom / clean

g) Helen / hair / blond / Diana / black

f) Davis / brother / tall / James / short

h) Daniel / pullover / white / Alfred / blue

FUN TIME

1 Word wheel.

Escreva as letras das palavras seguindo a direção das flechas.

Depois junte as letras pintadas de amarelo (na ordem dos números) e você terá o nome de um grande piloto brasileiro de Fórmula 1.

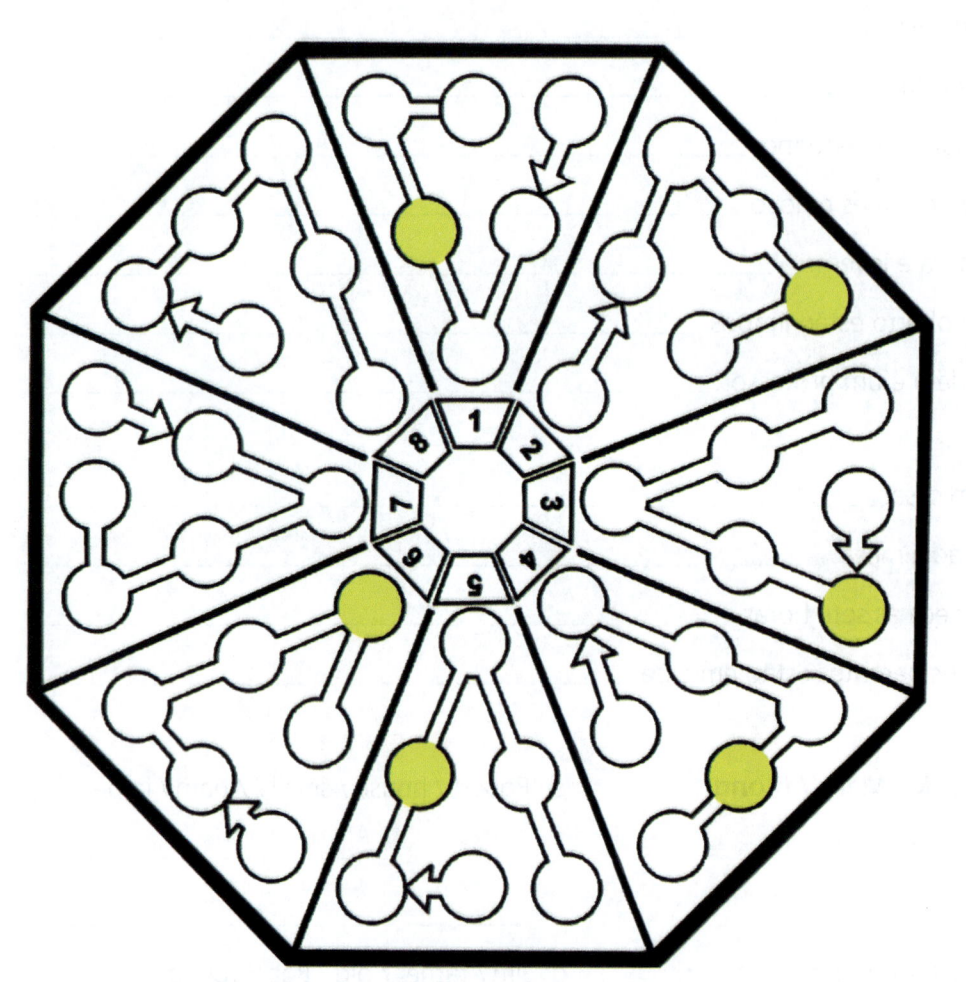

1. Galho
2. Irmã
3. Sempre
4. Quase
5. Blusa
6. Amigo
7. Motorista
8. Rodas

2 Pyramid translation.

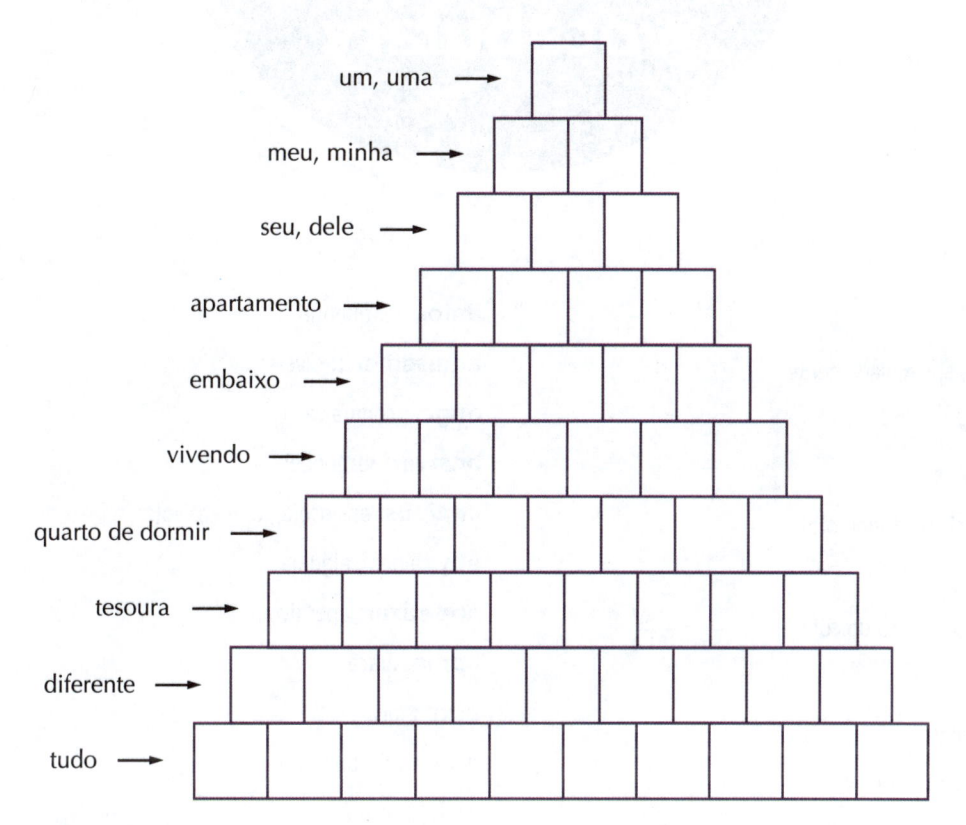

- um, uma
- meu, minha
- seu, dele
- apartamento
- embaixo
- vivendo
- quarto de dormir
- tesoura
- diferente
- tudo

LET'S SING

Silent night!

Silent night! Silent night!
Holy night!
All is calm. All is bright,
'round yon virgin Mother and Child.
Holy infant so tender and mild,
Sleep in heavenly peace,
Sleep in heavenly peace.

🔘 23

Word bank

silent: silencioso, quieto
holy: santo, sagrado
bright: brilhante, luminoso
'round (around): em volta, em torno
yon: lá, aquele, aquela (forma antiga de younder: lá, acolá)
tender: tenro, delicado
mild: meigo
heavenly: celestial
peace: paz

General vocabulary

A

about: sobre, aproximadamente
above: acima
absent: ausente
absent-minded: distraído(a)
actor: ator
according to: de acordo com
actress: atriz
admire: admirar
advice: conselho, aviso
afraid: com medo
after: depois
afternoon: tarde
agency: agência
ago: atrás, antes
agree: concordar
ahead: em frente
air conditioning: ar-condicionado
alarm clock: despertador
all: tudo, todo
all right: tudo bem
almost: quase
alone: sozinho(a)
along: ao longo de
a lot of: uma porção de
aloud: em voz alta
also: também
always: sempre
among: entre (muitos)

amount: quantia
amusement: diversão
angry: com raiva
answer: responder
anxious: ansioso(a), apreensivo(a)
any: algum, alguma
appetizer: aperitivo
apple: maçã
arm: braço
armchair: poltrona
article: artigo
around: ao redor de
arrive: chegar
ash: cinza
ashtray: cinzeiro
ask: perguntar, pergunte
attend: frequentar
attentive: atento(a)
aunt: tia
autumn (fall): outono
awful: horrível

B

baby: bebê
back: atrás, de volta
bad: ruim, mau
bag: mala
baker: padeiro
barbecue: churrasco
bark: latir

basket: cesta
be: ser, estar
beach: praia
beautiful: bonito(a)
beauty: beleza
be back: estar de volta, voltar
because: porque
bed: cama
bedroom: quarto de dormir
bedside table: criado-mudo
before: antes de
begin: começar
behind: atrás de
bell: campainha
belly: barriga
belong: pertencer
belt: cinto
bench: banco
best: melhor
between: entre (dois)
big: grande
birthday: aniversário
black: preto(a)
blackboard: lousa
blanket: cobertor
blanks: claros
block: quadra, quarteirão
blond: loiro(a)
blow: soprar
blue: azul
body: corpo
book: livro
bookcase: estante de livros
booklet: livreto
bookshop: livraria
boot: bota
box: caixa, quadro

branch: galho
Brazilian: brasileiro(a)
bread: pão
breakfast: café da manhã
breeze: brisa
bright: brilho
brightly: brilhantemente
bring: trazer
brother: irmão
brush: escova, escovar
build: construir
building: edifício, construindo
bus: ônibus
but: mas
butter: manteiga
buy: comprar
by: por

C

cake: bolo
call: chamar, telefonar
camera: máquina fotográfica
can: poder (v.)
cannot (can't): não pode
cap: boné
cards: cartas
carpenter: carpinteiro
carpet: carpete, tapete
carry: carregar
cashier: caixa, contador(a)
cart: carroça
cat: gato(a)
catch: pegar, agarrar
cause: causar
celebrate: celebrar
chair: cadeira
chalk: giz

chalkboard: quadro-negro
change: mudar, trocar; troco
chart: mapa, gráfico, tabela
chatterer: tagarela
cheap: barato
chest: peito
child: criança, filho(a)
chin: queixo
children: crianças; filhos
church: igreja
class: classe
classmate: colega de classe
classroom: sala de aula
clean: limpo; limpar
clerk: empregado, balconista
clock: relógio de parede
close: fechar
clothes: roupas
cloud: nuvem
cloudy: nublado
clue: dica, pista
coat: paletó, sobretudo
coat hanger: cabideiro
coffee: café
cold: frio
color: cor, colorir
comb: pentear, pente
come: vir
come back: voltar
comfortable: confortável
common: comum
company: companhia
computer: computador
congratulations: parabéns
contribute: contribuir
cook: cozinhar; cozinheiro(a)
cool: legal, bacana

corner: canto, esquina
cost: custar
country: país
course (of course): certamente
course: curso
cousin: primo
cow: vaca
cowboy: vaqueiro
crazy: maluco(a), doido(a)
crawl: rastejar, arrastar
cross: cruzar, atravessar; cruz
crowded: cheio(a), lotado(a), apinhado(a)
cry: chorar, gritar
cup: xícara
cut: cortar
cycle: andar de bicicleta

D

dad: pai
daddy: papai
daily: diário
data: dados
dancer: dançarino(a)
danger: perigo
dangerous: perigoso(a)
day: dia
dear: querido(a)
death: morte
decorate: enfeitar, decorar
degree: grau
deliverer: entregador(a)
delivery: entrega
dentist's: consultório dentário
deserve: merecer
diary: diário
difficult: difícil
dinner: jantar, janta

direction: direção, orientação
dirty: sujo(a)
disappear: desaparecer
discover: descobrir
distract: distrair
do: fazer, realizar
does: faz
dog: cão
doing: fazendo
doll: boneca
donkey: macaco(a)
door: porta
dot: ponto
down: baixo
draw: desenhar
drawer: gaveta
dressing table: penteadeira
drink: beber, bebida
drive: dirigir
driver: motorista
driver's license: carteira de motorista
driving school: escola de trânsito
duck: pato
during: durante

E

ear: orelha, ouvido
early: cedo
easy: fácil
eat: comer
echo: eco
educated: educado(a)
employee: empregado
empty: vazio(a)
end: fim
end: terminar, acabar
engineer: engenheiro(a)

England: Inglaterra
English: inglês
enjoy: desfrutar, apreciar
erase: apagar
eraser: borracha
escape: escapar
evening: tarde; anoitecer
every: cada
everybody: todos
everything: tudo
everywhere: em toda parte
eye: olho
excuse me: desculpe-me
exercise: exercício
expensive: caro(a)
experience: experiência
explosion: explosão
explosive: explosivo

F

factory: fábrica
fail: falhar, falta
fair: feira; bonito(a), elegante
fall: cair; outono
falling: caindo
famous: famoso
far from: longe de
farm: fazenda
farmer: fazendeiro(a)
fast: rápido(a)
fasten: apertar, prender
fat: gordo(a)
father: pai
fence: cerca
field: campo
file: ficha
fill in: preencher

find: encontrar
fine: bem, bom, ótimo
finger: dedo
finish: terminar
fireman: bombeiro
fireplace: lareira
first: primeiro(a)
first of all: antes de tudo
fish: peixe
fisher: pescador
fisherman: pescador
fix: consertar
flag: bandeira
flash: brilho
flat: apartamento
floor: chão, piso, andar
flower: flor
food: comida
follow: seguir, siga
for: para, por
forest: floresta
forget: esquecer
foot: pé
forty: quarenta
fox: raposa
free: livre
freezing: gelado
frequently: frequentemente
fresh: fresco
Friday: sexta-feira
friend: amigo(a)
friendship: amizade
from: de, desde (origem)
frozen: gelado
fruit: fruta, frutas
full: cheio(a)
fun: divertimento
funny: divertido(a), engraçado(a)

G

game: jogo
garden: jardim
gardener: jardineiro
gas station: posto de gasolina
geese: gansos
generally: geralmente
get: conseguir, ter, comprar
get off the bus: descer do ônibus
get on the bus: subir no ônibus
get up: levantar
girl: menina, moça
give: dar
given: dado
glass: copo, vidro
glasses: óculos
glue: cola
go: ir
go away: ir embora
God: Deus
goes: vai (v. 3ª p. sing.)
going: indo
good: bom
goose: ganso
go out: sair
grandfather: avô
grandmother: avó
grass: grama
great: grande; ótimo(a)
greedy: ávido(a)
green: verde
guide: guia

H

had: tinha, teve...
hair: cabelo

hand: mão
happy: feliz
hard: duro(a)
hardworking: trabalhador(a), esforçado(a)
has: tem (v. 3ª p. sing.)
has got: tem
hat: chapéu
hate: detestar
have: ter, tenha
have (have got): ter
head: cabeça
healthy: saudável
help: ajudar; socorro
hen: galinha
her: dela
hero: heroi
here: aqui
here you are: aqui está
here you have: aqui está, aqui você tem
hey: ei
hidden: escondido(a)
his: dele
hit: bater
hold: segurar
holiday: férias, feriado
home: casa, lar
homework: tarefa de casa
hot: quente
house: casa
housewife: dona de casa
how: como
how old: que idade
how many: quantos
how much: quanto
hundred: cem
hungry: faminto(a)
husband: marido

I

ice cream: sorvete
idle: preguiçoso(a)
impobilite: mal-educado
impossible: impossível
I'm sorry: sinto muito
in front of: na frente de
injury: machucar
interesting: interessante
interpreter: intérprete
interview: entrevista, entrevistar
introduce: apresentar
it: ele, ela
its: seu, sua, dele, dela
it's: é, está
it's going to rain: vai chover
it's your turn: é sua vez
invite: convidar
I've got: tenho
I was born: eu nasci

J

job: trabalho, emprego
join: unir, juntar
joke: piada, anedota
juice: suco
jump: pular
jumper: pulador; tipo de blusa
just: justo, exatamente

K

keep calm: ficar calmo(a)
key: chave
kick: chute
kind: espécie, tipo; bondoso(a)
kitchen: cozinha
knee: joelho

knife: faca
knives: facas
know: conhecer

L

lady: dama, senhora
lake: lago
law: lei
lawyer: advogado(a)
large: grande, espaçoso(a)
last: último; durar
last name: sobrenome
late: atrasado(a); tarde
later: mais tarde
laugh: rir, gargalhar
lazy: preguiçoso(a)
leaf: folha
leaflet: folheto
leave: deixar, partir
leaves: folhas
left: partiu, deixou
leg: perna
less: menos
lesson: lição, aula
let: permitir deixar
letter: carta, letra
let's: vamos
let's go: vamos
library: biblioteca
life: vida
lift: levantar
like: gostar; como (comparativo)
listen to: escutar
little: pequeno; pouco
live: morar, viver
living room: sala de estar
look: olhar

look at: olhar para
lose: perder
lost: perdido (a)
loud: alto (som)
loudly: em som alto
love: amar; amor
lovely: amável, adorável
low: baixo
lunch: almoço, lanche

M

magazine: revista
mail: correio
mailman: carteiro
major: maior, major (militar)
make: fazer, fabricar
make the bed: arrumar a cama
man: homem
manager: gerente
many: muitos, muitas
market: mercado
marvelous: maravilhoso(a)
match: partida; fósforo; combinar, unir
may: posso, pode...
me: me, mim
meal: refeição
meaning: significado
meet: encontrar (pessoas)
men: homens
mess: bagunça
message: mensagem
mice: ratos
midday: meio-dia
midnight: meia-noite
milk: leite; ordenhar
mirror: espelho
missing: que falta; ausente; desaparecido

mistake: erro, falha
mom: mãe
money: dinheiro
monkey: macaco
month: mês
moon: lua
moonlight: luz da lua
more: mais
morning: manhã
mother: mãe
mouse: rato
mouth: boca
move: mudar, movimentar, mexer
movies: cinema
much: muito
must: precisa, deve

N
napkin: guardanapo
nature: natureza
native: nativo(a)
near: perto
neck: pescoço
necklace: colar
need: precisar
neighbour: vizinho(a)
new: novo
news: notícia, novidade
newspaper: jornal
next: próximo
nice: bonito, ótimo
nice to meet you: prazer em conhecê-lo(a)
night: noite
no: não; nenhum
noon: meio-dia
normally: normalmente
nose: nariz
noun: nome, substantivo

now: agora
number: número
nurse: enfermeira

O
obey: obedecer
observer: observador(a)
ocean: oceano
occupation: ocupação, profissão
occur: ocorrer, acontecer
o'clock: em ponto
of: de
of course: naturalmente, claro
off: fora
office: escritório
old: velho(a)
on: à, em, no, na...
once more: uma vez mais
only: somente
open: abrir; aberto
opponent: adversário(a)
or: ou
orange: laranja (fruta e cor)
orange juice: suco de laranja
orchard: pomar
other: outro(a)
our: nosso(a)
out: fora
ox: boi
oxen: bois

P
page: página
paint: pintar; tinta
pants: calça
papaya: mamão
paper basket: cesta de lixo para papel

party: festa
pass: passar
pay: pagar
pay attention: preste atenção
peach: pêssego
peel: descascar
pen: caneta
pencil: lápis
people: pessoas, povo
perform: realizar, fazer, desempenhar
photograph: foto
pick up: pegar, apanhar
picture: pintura, quadro, figura
pie: empada, torta
pig: porco
pillow: travesseiro
place: lugar
plate: prato
play: jogar, brincar, tocar instrumento
player: jogador(a)
pleasant: agradável
please: por favor
pleasure: prazer
point: apontar
policeman: policial
policemen: policiais
polite: educado(a), polido(a)
poor: pobre
popcorn: pipoca
postcard: cartão-postal
postman: carteiro
post office: correio
pot: vaso
potato: batata
power: poder, força
power station: estação de força
practical: prático

practice: praticar, pratique
proper: próprio(a)
property: propriedade
protect: proteger
pull: puxe, puxar
push: empurrar
put: pôr, colocar

R

rain: chuva, chover
rainy: chuvoso(a)
raise: levantar
reach: alcançar, chegar
read: ler
ready: pronto(a)
really: realmente
rearrange: rearranjar
reason: razão, motivo
recess time: recreio, intervalo
red: vermelho
relatives: parentes
research: pesquisa
repair: consertar
responsible: responsável
rest: descansar
return: retornar, volta
rewrite: reescrever
rice: arroz
rich: rico(a)
right: direito, certo, correto
ring: tocar campainha; anel
road: estrada
rocky: rochedo
room: sala
rope: corda
run: correr
running: correndo

S

sail: navegar, andar de barco
sailor: marinheiro
salesman: vendedor
same: mesmo
Saturday: sábado
sea: mar
search: procurar, procura
season: estação
seat: assento
seat belt: cinto de segurança
severe: severo(a)
school: escola
secretary: secretária
see: ver, veja
see you later: até mais tarde
sell: vender
send: enviar
serious: sério(a)
sing: cantar
sit down: sentar
shark: tubarão
sheep: ovelha, ovelhas
shelf: prateleira, estante
shine: brilhar
ship: navio
shirt: camisa
shoe: sapato
shop: loja, fazer compras
short: curto; baixo
shout: gritar
show: mostrar; espetáculo
showed: mostrava, mostrou
shower: banho de chuveiro
shut: fechar
sign: sinal

silly: bobo(a)
sing: cantar
singer: cantor(a)
sister: irmã
sit: sentar
sit down: sentar
sitting: sentado, sentando
skirt: saia
sky: céu
sleep: dormir
slim: magro(a)
slip: escorregar
slippers: chinelos
slippery: escorregadio
slow: vagoroso(a), lento(a)
slowly: devagar
small: pequeno(a)
smart: esperto(a), inteligente
smile: sorriso, sorrir
smoke: fumar, fumaça
snack: petisco, lanche leve
snake: cobra
snow: neve; nevar
snowy: com neve, nevado
so: tão; por isso
socks: meias (curtas)
some: algum, alguma, alguns, algumas
something: algo, alguma coisa
son: filho
song: canção
soon: logo
sorry (I'm sorry): sinto muito, desculpe
speak: falar
speaker: locutor(a)
speed: velocidade
spend: passar, gastar
spoon: colher

spot: ponto, apontar
spring: primavera
stadium: estádio
stand: barraca; ficar
stand up: ficar de pé
start: começar
state: estado
station: estação
stay: ficar
stool: banquinho, tamborete
stop: parar
storm: tempestade
stormy: tempestuoso
story: história
strange: estranho
street: rua
strict: severo(a)
strong: forte
study: estudar
subject: assunto
such as: assim como
summer: verão
Sun: Sol
sunshine: brilho do sol
sunny: ensolarado, com sol
supporter: torcedor(a)
suppose: supor
sure: certo, claro, seguramente
surname: sobrenome
sweater: suéter
sweet: doce
swim: nadar
swimmer: nadador(a)
swimming pool: piscina

T

table: mesa, quadro
take: pegar, tomar, levar

take off: tirar, decolar
talk: falar
tall: alto(a)
tea: chá
teach: ensinar
teacher: professor(a)
team: time
Teddy bear: ursinho de pelúcia
teeth: dentes
tell: contar, dizer
tennis shoes: tênis
thank you = thanks: obrigado(a)
that: aquele, aquela, aquilo
that's fine: está ótimo
their: deles, delas
them: os, as, lhes
then: então, depois
there: lá
there are: há (plural)
there is: há (singular)
there was: havia (singular)
there were: havia (plural)
these: estes, estas
thick: grosso(a), espesso(a)
thief: ladrão
thin: magro(a), fino(a)
thing: coisa
think: pensar
third: terceiro(a)
thirty: trinta
this: este, esta, isto
those: aqueles, aquelas
throw: jogar, arremessar
time: tempo, vez
tired: cansado(a)
to: para
tobacco: tabaco, fumo

today: hoje
toe: dedo do pé
tomato: tomate
tomorrow: amanhã
ton: tonelada
too: também
too much: demais
tooth: dente
topaz: topázio
touch: tocar
tour agency: agência de turismo
tour guide: guia de turismo
towel: toalha
town: cidade (pequena, média)
toy: brinquedo
traffic laws: leis do trânsito
traffic sign: sinal de trânsito
traffic light: farol de trânsito
train: trem
translate: traduzir
travel: viajar, viagem
treat: tratar
tree: árvore
trip: viagem
trousers: calça
truck: caminhão
T-shirt: camiseta
turn: virar
turn right: vire à direita
turn left: vire à esquerda

U
ugly: feio(a)
uncle: tio
under: debaixo
unemployed: desempregado(a)
unpleasant: desagradável

until: até
up: para cima; de pé
usually: usualmente, geralmente

V
vacation: férias
vegetable: legume
very: muito
very much: muitíssimo
village: aldeia, povoação
view: vista, panorama
voice: voz

W
wait: esperar
waiter: garçom
waitress: garçonete
walk: caminhar, andar
wall: parede, muro
want: querer, desejar
war: guerra
wardrobe: guarda-roupa
warm: quente
was: era, estava
wash: lavar
waste: desperdiçar
wasted: desperdiçado, rejeitado
wastebasket: cesto de lixo
watch: assistir, olhar; relógio de pulso
watching: vendo
water: água
way: caminho (this way: dessa maneira)
weak: fraco(a), débil
wear: usar (roupas)
weather: tempo (temperatura)
week: semana
weekend: fim de semana

welcome: bem-vindo
welcome: dar as boas-vindas, receber
well: bem
wet: úmido(a), molhado(a)
what: o quê, qual
what about: que tal?
what a pity: que pena
what do you do?: o que você faz?
what time is it?: que horas são?
what's she like?: Como ela é?
what's the (park) like?: como é (o parque)?
wheel: roda
when: quando
when were you born?: quando você nasceu?
where: onde, para onde
where are you from?: de onde você é?
whistle: apito, assobio
who: quem
who are you?: quem é você?
who's: quem é, quem está
why: por que
why not?: por que não?
white: branco(a)
wife: esposa
wild: selvagem
wind: vento
windy: com vento

window: janela
winter: inverno
with: com
without: sem
wives: esposas
wolf: lobo
woman: mulher
women: mulheres
wonderful: maravilhoso(a)
word: palavra
work: trabalhar, trabalho
worker: operário, trabalhador
wow: oba
write: escrever
writer: escritor(a)
writing desk: escrivaninha
wrong: errado
why?: por que (pergunta)

Y

yard: pátio, quintal
year: ano
yellow: amarelo
yesterday: ontem
you: você, vocês
young: jovem
your: seu
you're welcome: de nada